TH

D0357009

Maxwell Maltz, M.D., F.I.C.S., discovered
the incredible powers of the hidden
self-image through his works as a
world-famous surgeon. He noticed
that many people who don't really need it
seek plastic surgery. Over the years
he realized that these people's real problem
was not their outward, physical image,
but their inner, hidden self-image. These
people were unhappy and unsuccessful because
their hidden self-images compelled them
to make mistakes, actually to do the wrong
thing. Subconsciously these people were
not aware that their self-images were
the cause of their failure. They hoped that
plastic surgery would change their self-image.
But, Dr. Maltz discovered that even if
he did perform surgery, these people were as
miserable, as defeated, as ever.

To help them, he developed the
mental exercises and other techniques
he gives you in this book. The exercises were
so successful, worked such miracles,
that Dr. Maltz felt compelled to
present his finding to the world.

Books by Maxwell Maltz

Creative Living for Today
The Magic Power of Self-Image Psychology
Psycho-Cybernetics
Psycho-Cybernetic Principles for Creative Living
Thoughts to Live By

Published by POCKET BOOKS

Most Pocket Books are available at special quantity discounts for bulk purchases for sales promotions, premiums or fund raising. Special books or book excerpts can also be created to fit specific needs.

For details write the office of the Vice President of Special Markets, Pocket Books, 1230 Avenue of the Americas, New York, New York 10020.

Dr. Maxwell Maltz

THE MAGIC POWER OF SELF-IMAGE PSYCHOLOGY

The New Way to a Bright, Full Life

PUBLISHED BY POCKET BOOKS NEW YORK

POCKET BOOKS, a division of Simon & Schuster, Inc.
1230 Avenue of the Americas, New York, N.Y 10020

Copyright © 1964 by Dr. Maxwell Maltz

Published by arrangement with Prentice-Hall, Inc.
Library of Congress Catalog Card Number: 64-20749

ISBN: 0-671-55595-2

First Pocket Books printing November, 1970

23   22   21   20   19   18   17

POCKET and colophon are registered trademarks
of Simon & Schuster, Inc.

Printed in the U.S.A.

Building a New World Within You

My aim in writing this book is very definite: I hope to help you, each of you, to reach out toward happier, more productive lives. If you let me help you and if your desire for the good life is strong, you will find that your horizons are brighter than you ever dreamed.

Life should be an exciting adventure. The sun should rise within you each day in terms of the richness of your feelings and the sharpness of your perceptions. You should carve out goals for yourself that will inspire you to enthusiastic action. Going toward life with vigor, no matter what your age, you should never fear death.

One of the greatest adventures in living is getting to know yourself better. It is a tragedy that some individuals spend a lifetime going nowhere, bogged down in frustration, because they don't know anything about themselves or how to cope with problems, many created by environment.

If you read this book thoughtfully, it will be a voyage of discovery for you. You will learn more about yourself and you will learn ways to improve yourself. I've included seven practice exercises and a number of specific suggestions to help you in your quest.

Americans spend enormous sums of money each year for material goods, and they can serve positive purposes. Houses, automobiles, furniture, clothes—they brighten our lives. Still, vastly more important is our thinking—especially our thinking about ourselves. This book revolves around this concept, around our self-image and how we can improve it.

As you read on, you will be amazed as you understand the incredible power of your self-image, the overwhelming impact it has on your destiny as a human being. I first understood this while engaged in my lifelong practice as a plastic surgeon and I am happy to share my ideas with you.

You will draw on a great treasure house to lead you onward —your imagination. From its vaults you will bring forth mental pictures and prop them up in the playhouse of your mind. We will watch the dramas together and learn valuable lessons from them.

This power of imaging is fantastic. Sometimes you may refuse to believe just how important it is but, beyond any doubt, it can predetermine successes and failures.

Some people short-change themselves and never reach their full share of possible accomplishments, or their full potential as human beings. If *you* emphasize your negative qualities and fail to appreciate your assets, we'll do something about it. If you are willing to exert effort in the best cause you'll ever have, you'll learn to be fair to yourself.

God brought us forth on this earth to *live,* not to stagnate. He meant us to be happy, to enjoy our lives. He meant us to relish every moment, to weave loving care on every day that we live—no matter how young or how old we are.

Happiness is a habit, just as is brushing your teeth or washing your face. *You can acquire this habit.* If you have been conditioned to feel sour about yourself and your world, you can change; you can take hold of this habit of happiness. These are not "just words." I know people who have changed, adventuring into a world unknown to them; the wonderful world of inner happiness.

I hope you'll allow me to help you in this direction—toward happiness.

MAXWELL MALTZ, M.D.

Contents

CONTENTS

Your Self-Image
Can Give You a Starring Role
on Life's Stage

Imagine that you are seated in a theatre, looking at the curtain which hides the blank screen, as you wait for the feature picture to begin.

What will this picture do for you? How will it affect you? What impact will it have on your life?

Will you feel moved—perhaps even to tears? Will you laugh at a comedy, or feel terrified at the crises faced by the hero or heroine? Will you feel wonderful waves of love and compassion—or surges of resentment?

All these feelings will pulse through you—and more. For the picture you will see is about the most fascinating person in the world—*yourself*.

In this theatre, which is in the mind and heart of each of us, you are the producer, director, writer, actor or actress, hero *and* the villain. You are the film technician up in the booth—and the audience which reacts to this thrilling drama.

The exciting story unfolding upon this inner screen is one which is invented every second of your life—yesterday, tomorrow, but most important, right now.

You watch the image upon that screen and you invent the image upon that screen—right now.

Will the story have a happy ending? Is it full of happiness and success or sorrow and failure? The story line is already there and the discerning eye can tell the direction in which the story will go.

But one realization can comfort you. Since you are the dramatist, the director, and the actor, you can change the story as it unfolds. Now. This instant. And for your whole lifetime.

You can make this a success story. You can be the hero and conquer the villain. And you can make this a heart-warming story which will enrich the lives of all who know you—rather than a drab mechanical tale, a chronicle of boredom.

It's all inside you.

It all depends on what you do with an image you carry inside you, an image which is your most important tool for good or for ill.

It all depends on you—and your self-image.

Making a Motion Picture—of Yourself

Now, what do we mean by the self-image? Is there such a thing?

We know there is a mind, even though no one has ever seen it. I don't mean a brain, which we can see. But the mind, which thinks, hopes, fears, grows happy, becomes sad, remembers, envisions, which invents molehills—and mountains.

The mind has just as much reality as the brain—even if we can't touch, feel, or see the mind.

And the self-image has reality, even if we can't touch, feel, or see it. In the pages of this book we will come to grips with this reality. Because success is real—and failure is real. Energy is real—and lassitude is real.

I will help you to use your self-image to develop the picture you've always wanted to see—a picture of you surmounting difficulties and driving on to a successful, happy conclusion.

Why is the self-image so important?

As I explained in my previous book *Psycho-Cybernetics*, the self-image is your own conception of the sort of person you are. It is a product of past experiences, successes and failures, humiliations, and triumphs, and the way other people react to you, especially in early childhood. From these factors, and from others which we shall discuss later, you build up a picture of yourself which you believe is true. The picture may be false—and in many cases *is* false—but the important fact here is that you act *just as if it were true*. For all intents and purposes, it *is* true.

"Then," you ask, "in that case, my picture of myself as a weakling, as a victim, the person to whom everything happens is true! What comfort is that?"

There is a wonderful comfort in one fact, embodied in two little words—"*as if.*" You see, I said you act *as if* the picture were true. But is it? Since this picture, self-image, can change and *has* been changed in thousands of cases, there is no cause for despair.

Understand this: *You* are the writer; *you* are the director; *you* are the actor starring in this picture.

All you have to learn is how to change that picture by investing a little more time and energy in it, by following time-proved methods which are so easy and so close to each of us that it's no wonder we've overlooked them. It just takes a new insight.

There's a story told about the famous Russian philosopher and mystic, Ouspensky. In order to pursue his researches into the nature of consciousness, he was forced to take a drug. While under the influence of this narcotic, he suddenly realized that he had found the secret of existence, that it had come from his subconscious where it had been all his life, and was there in simple terms, released by the drug. Eagerly, he seized a pencil and wrote down the wonderful formula for success. Then he dropped off into a deep sleep.

On waking up, completely conscious now, he examined the precious piece of paper. There, scrawled in his own handwriting, he saw the words: "Think . . . in new categories."

This is what I hope to help you do. Think, feel, act in new categories. Re-examine what you've taken for granted. Become dissatisfied with "proof." Broaden your beliefs. In other words, change your self-image.

We will work together to change this mental picture of yourself. We will discuss the factors that go to make up this self-image. Over and over, because concentration is necessary, we will use the powerful tool of mental picturing to redefine your concept of yourself, to enhance the appreciation of the unique individual that you are, each of you.

Words are not enough. In the pages of this book you will find seven practice exercises, exercises in imagination, each of which will help you break through the barrier of your previous limitations. The power of mental picturing will help you burst through the self-imposed obstacles that are blocking your dreams.

These exercises can be the most important ones you've ever worked on. I planned them carefully to help you see yourself new, on the rise, going forward to realistic successes that are within your grasp.

Don't defeat yourself by feeling skeptical about these exercises! They are not tangible, you cannot reach out and touch the concepts in them, as you would a chair or a table. But the images you will see, the pictures of anticipation you will manufacture—these are products of rare power. This power of your mind pictures is awesome; it may be difficult for you to understand the impact of their power. Perhaps you must have *faith*. I hope you will, because I can help you so much.

Aside from these exercises, I will offer you specific suggestions for living happily in this difficult age, ideas which will help you to feel more kindly about the only self you've got.

Your Mental Blueprint

Certainly the discovery of the self-image is one of the most important finds of this century. For, though we may not realize it, we all do carry with us this mental blueprint or picture of ourselves. We may not be conscious of it, but it exists. We believe firmly in it and do not question its validity.

Furthermore, all our actions and emotions are consistent with our self-image. You will act like the sort of person you think you are. You simply can't act otherwise, even if you exercise all your will power. The man who thinks he is a "failure type" person will find a way to fail, no matter how hard he tries to succeed, even if a few good breaks do come his way. The person who thinks he's just "unlucky" will manage to prove that he is indeed a victim of "bad luck."

The self-image is the foundation stone of our whole personality. Because of this, our experiences seem to verify, and thereby strengthen our self-images, setting up a vicious (or pleasant) cycle.

A salesman who thinks he is unworthy will face his prospect with a dejected expression. He will almost apologize for his very existence, literally inviting rejection. He will shake the confidence of the prospective buyer and he will have "proof" that his self-image is correct; he is unlovable, inferior, and a failure.

The high school girl who thinks she is ugly and unattractive to boys will find a way to prove that her self-image is accurate. If a boy tells her she has a nice figure, she will think of the mole on her cheek. If told she has pretty eyes, she will tell herself that her nose is too long. Her hang-dog, defensive manner will eventually drive her potential admirers away, and she will have found confirmation that her way of seeing herself, as ugly, is true.

You Can Change Your Self-Image

Because of this so-called "objective truth," the person rarely realizes that the trouble lies in his own evaluation of himself. If you tell the salesman that he only *thinks* he cannot sell, he will look at you skeptically. He knows only that he has tried and tried, but where are the results? If you tell the girl that she is really quite attractive, she will also try to prove you wrong. After all, she has no boy friends!

Yet—and I will tell you true life stories of real people— salesmen have made almost miraculous changes in earning capacity; and defensive, almost antisocial girls have adapted beautifully to boys—when they understood the importance of changing their self-image.

For, this is basic, *the self-image can be changed*. One is never too young nor too old to change his self-image and start a new, more productive, more creative life.

In the past, it has seemed difficult for a person to change his basic habits because his main effort has been directed at the circumference of the self, rather than at the very core. Many people have tried to use "positive thinking" to conquer some external obstacle or character defect ("I will relax more next week," "I will pass the examination"). But they had not tried to change their thinking about the self that was to do these things.

"Positive thinking" can be used as a kind of crutch for the same old self-image—but it will not be really effective. For, how can one think positively about some situation, if one carries with him a negative opinion about his very self? A basic conflict is set up here. But, many experiments have shown that once the idea of self is changed, other things consistent with this new concept may be accomplished—often without great strain.

Prescott Lecky, a pioneer in self-image psychology, made some convincing experiments. He regarded the personality as a system of ideas, all of which must *seem* to be consistent with each other. Ideas inconsistent with the system are rejected, he believed, while those which *seem* consistent are accepted. At the center of this system of ideas is the person's "self-image," his conception of himself. A schoolteacher, Lecky was able to test his theory on thousands of pupils. (*Self Consistency, a Theory of Personality,* The Island Press, New York, N.Y.)

Lecky believed that if a student had difficulty learning a subject, it could be because, from the student's point of view, learning it would be inconsistent for him. However, he reasoned, if you change the student's self-conception underlying this attitude, he would be able to look at the subject differently. If the student would change his self-definition, he could also change his learning ability. This proved to be so.

One student who was a poor speller and failed so many subjects that he lost credit for a year, made an excellent grade the next year and became one of the school's best spellers. Another boy, dropped from the college because of poor grades, became an "A" student at one of the country's most respected universities. A girl who had failed Latin four times finished with a fine grade after receiving guidance. A boy, told by a testing bureau he had no aptitude for English, won honorable mention the next year for a literary prize.

These students were neither stupid nor lacking in basic aptitude. Suffering from inadequate self-images, they identified with their failures. When they failed a test or a subject, they classified themselves generally as "failures." Their change in self-conception merely released latent abilities.

Lecky, using the same method, cured students of nail-biting and stuttering.

My own files contain equally convincing case histories:

The schoolteacher who had to drag herself out of bed to face her class each day; now, seeing herself more accurately, she enjoys relating to her pupils. The movie star whose frayed nerves were forcing her into semi-retirement; today, unafraid to expose her feelings, she faces the camera without panic. The executive whose timidity interfered with his work responsibilities; today he likes himself and because of this, other people at the office find him relaxing.

These are true stories. Other people, struggling human beings like you, have changed their pictures of themselves—and their lives. So can you!

Discoveries of a Plastic Surgeon

At first glance, one would think there was little connection between plastic surgery and psychology. Yet it was my work as a plastic surgeon which first made me realize the existence of the self-image, raising questions which led to important psychological conclusions.

For, upon starting the practice of plastic surgery many years ago, I was amazed by the dramatic, sudden changes in personality which often took place when a facial defect was corrected. In many cases changing the physical image seemed to create an entirely new person. My scalpel often seemed to have magical powers, capable not only of improving the patient's appearance, but of transforming his whole outlook on life. Fearful people became bold, the angry became friendly, the self-effacing were now outgoing.

A "mean," aggressive adolescent boy, who always fought with his schoolmates, won the acceptance of his peers when he dropped his defenses and just tried to be friendly.

A listless middle-aged man who was just going through the motions felt new hope rise within him; his once despairing eyes mirrored a life they had not shown in many years.

Explaining the successes was easy. For example, the girl

with the harelip, who had been teased about it all her life by her classmates. She had felt inferior about it; her thinking was negative. She was obsessed by the thought that none of her friends had a harelip. That was her trouble, she thought, the harelip. Why shouldn't she feel afraid of attack? She stood out because of her physical defect, was a natural target for the cruel. When her harelip was corrected by surgery, why shouldn't she feel less defensive, more hopeful in her thinking and in her concept of self? That she improved emotionally was no surprise.

But what about the exceptions who didn't change—even after their features were improved by surgery?

Yes, as a plastic surgeon, it was my "failures" that really taught me the vast importance of a person's self-image for, when I improved a person's physical features without an accompanying lift in his spirits, I had to ask myself what was wrong.

One day many years ago a woman in her mid-twenties came to my offices. She had a deep indented scar on her left cheek, a constant reminder of an automobile accident she'd been in. She looked unhappy, with herself and her life.

"Who wouldn't be, in her situation," I asked myself. "As a kid, looking in the mirror when she brushed her teeth or combed her hair, she saw a perfectly normal face and began to take it for granted. Now, when she looks in the mirror, she must think, 'Gosh, I look awful! I used to have a normal face, now I have two entirely different cheeks.'"

I told her that I'd remove the scar and, after surgery, she'd look fine once again. "Don't worry," I said. "We'll take good care of you."

She asked how she would look, and I reassured her and tried to soothe her fears. Later, I operated on her.

After a week's time, she came back. I took the bandages off and handed her a mirror. Her scarred cheek was a thing of the past.

Then I waited for her reaction. Many patients are overjoyed when they first see their new, improved image. But her reaction was uncertain; she expressed no real positive emotion.

I waited a few seconds, then said, "What do you think? Do you like it?"

She responded, "I really don't see any improvement."

I was stunned. My surgery had been totally successful. "Would you like to see the pictures of your face before the operation?"

She looked at the "before" pictures, then surveyed her new face in the hand mirror. "It looks better," she admitted, "but I don't *feel* better!"

Cases such as this one (and there have been many!) helped me to understand that all our scars cannot be seen, that some are worse than physical scars, that they are deep inside us, and infinitely painful.

Upon talking to this young woman, I learned more about her inner, emotional scar—about an unhappy, frustrated romance which had ended two years before, many months before the automobile accident. The grief was still with her; her self-image was poor. She was still unhappy after the removal of her physical scar, which was comparatively superficial. She still longed for her lover, and felt that she could not be happy without him.

What could cure her? What could she hope for? Physically, she was young and attractive, but what could remove her despair? A changing, a strengthening of her self-image, of her *feeling* about herself! If she could improve her opinion about *herself*, she would feel renewed courage, would go out more confidently into the world, meet another fine young man, and work toward greater fulfillment of her natural life impulses.

Are You True to Yourself?

"This above all: to thine own self be true," wrote William Shakespeare many, many years ago.

But the fact is that quite a few people are not true to themselves. Like the girl whose case I've just told you about, they reject themselves. After surgery has dramatically improved their appearance, they negate the change, refuse to acknowledge it, insist that they look the same as they did before the operation. Showing them "before" and "after" photographs does no good; it even arouses anger.

For people's images of themselves—good, bad or neutral—depend on past successes and failures. This concept of one's own worth is so important, so much deeper and more meaningful than a mirror. People carry this self-image into present activities and into plans for the future too.

If one's self-image is nourished on past successes, it will be pleasant.

But if inhibitions have blocked off the road to success, and past failures clutter up the mind, one's self-image will be poor—as in the case of this girl whose case I have described.

What do you think of yourself? I mean, what do you *really* think of yourself, deep down inside? Do you like yourself, or do you regard yourself with distrust? Do you expect too much of yourself or do you sit back passively, waiting for life to come to you, for people *to do things for you?* Do you set reasonable goals for yourself, goals whose accomplishment will help you feel whole and alive or do you let other people tell you what to do, what to think, and how to behave? Do you think you are good-looking or do you secretly think of your too-long nose or your too-big mouth?

What you think is very important.

Many people, over the years, have come to my office complaining of defects that were purely imaginary, by-products of what these people *thought of themselves*.

There are the middle-aged women who are convinced they look "old" even though their appearance is normal and often very attractive. There are the young girls who are positive they are "ugly" just because physically they are not exact duplicates of the latest movie queen. There are men whose false beliefs about their physical image defeats their life goals.

These people are their own worst enemies; they think themselves into a living death.

How to Live Joyfully

How, then, does one live the happy life? How does one find joy living in this busy, complicated world of ours? What is the secret?

It is really so simple. To really "live," to find life enjoyable, you must have a realistic, adequate self-image, one that you can live *with*. You must like and trust yourself. You must feel that you can express yourself without fear of exposure; you

10

must feel no need to hide your true self. You must know yourself well. Your self-image must be realistic, what you really are. You feel good when your self-image is intact and adequate. You feel full of confidence. You are ready to show the world what you are. And you are proud of it. You breathe life, give deeply to life—and take happily from it.

When a facial defect is corrected by plastic surgery, dramatic psychological changes occur only if there is a corresponding change of the distorted self-image. Otherwise, the change is only superficial.

Make Friends with Yourself

So you, in the theatre, looking at yourself on stage where you will act out the concepts outlined in this book, take mirror in hand and look at yourself. Look long, and look deeply, and do not be afraid of what you will see.

Do you know how to look? What to look for?

Do I hear someone say, "I'll see myself"?

Will you? You will see someone with ears, eyes, nose, legs, arms, but is it these physical features that you are looking for?

No, look behind these features—to the inner face, emotions, beliefs, the hidden stranger within you, which you cannot see in a mirror.

This is your self-image.

If an enemy, your self-image uses the failures of the past to undermine you, to make you a failure in the present.

If a friend, it draws from the confidence of past successes to give you courage to live and grow.

Make friends with yourself! Only then will you be happy and attain status as a human being!

On this stage, in the playhouse of your mind, we will act out dramas in which you will be the central character, with your self-image as a friend.

"But," you may tell me, "I have no outer scar, my face is normal. Is this book for me?"

It certainly is. Less than one percent of the U.S. population has facial defects requiring plastic surgery; over 99 percent have normal faces. But of this 99 percent or so, many of you have scars within—distorted self-images. *So many of us sell ourselves short!*

In the pages of this book you will find practical suggestions for improving your self-image and exercises designed to accelerate your pattern of positive change. You will set for yourself the goals which you long to achieve—success, happiness, friends, money, relaxation, whatever they are—and, if they are reasonable goals, we will move toward them utilizing the power of mental imagery.

To improve your self-image, you must be willing to apply your mental energies in doing these vital practice exercises. If you work hard at them, you can change. More than that, the changes may seem miraculous to you and your friends. But you must work hard, stepping out on the stage of your mind to practice. Actor Laurence Olivier's superb craftsmanship did not just happen.

At first you will flub your lines and miss your cues—don't worry about it and don't blame yourself for it! Change takes time and effort. But if you keep at it, the production will be smooth later on.

Aldous Huxley, the great English writer, once wrote, "There's only one corner of the universe you can be certain of improving; and that's your own self."

That's just what we're going to do!

2

Truth and Imagination—
Keys to Your Personality

You are going to change your self-image. You are tired of tearing yourself down, heaping criticisms on your thoughts and actions. Perhaps you're still not convinced you're worth the trouble, but still you're determined to see yourself with pride. You will, too, if you're willing to work. I promise you that your mental picturing can be changed—and your life with it.

First, however, we must select the equipment we are going to use in this overhauling of your self-imagery.

Our first tool is extremely powerful. It is simply the truth.

"Ye shall know the truth, and the truth shall make you free" *(John* viii.32). "Truth crushed to earth shall rise again" (Bryant).

Yes, truth either sustains us or lets us down. Its importance in our lives is overwhelming.

What is the truth about yourself? Are you convinced that your image of yourself is a true one? Do you look at yourself as a fool, a buffoon? As a coward? A hero? A master of your fate—or a victim?

As you stand on the stage of life and look at yourself in the mirror, how do you judge yourself? What are your good points—and your bad? Do you like yourself? Are you a friend—or an enemy?

The most important exploration which faces mankind—and you, personally—today is not the exploration of outer space, but the exploration of *inner space*. It can change whole civilizations—and it can improve your life through the most rewarding adventure of your whole existence.

What Is the Real Truth about Yourself?

Did I hear you say, "Of course I know the truth about myself! If I don't know myself, who does?"

But psychologists and psychiatrists have repeatedly pointed out that the most difficult person for one to evaluate objectively is one's own self.

Surely, if you stop to think of people you know, you'll agree with me. All of us know intelligent people who think they are stupid, good-looking people who imagine themselves ugly, and people who downgrade themselves constantly, evaluating all successes as failures.

In my practice as a plastic surgeon, I have often met people whose self-evaluations were grossly inaccurate. One patient comes to mind, a timid teen-ager. His "truth" about himself was that he was weak, that his receding chin had doomed him to a life of misery.

When he first came to my office, he was 18, ready for college, but he didn't even want to go. He felt he was worthless. His high school record had been poor; he had listlessly dawdled his way through four boring years. He had taken part in no physical activities, had no real friends, kept to himself and died inside. Why should college be any better?

I was his last hope. Could I do anything with the chin with which Fate had saddled him?

Something was wrong with his self-image, I saw quickly, for though his chin was not classically perfect, it was no different from millions of other chins. These other millions of people surely did not give such a mild imperfection even a second thought. But he was obsessed with it.

The recession in his chin was too mild to require plastic surgery, so instead I talked to him about it. I asked him when he had first begun to worry about his chin and why he associated it with weakness.

After seeing him several times, I got the full story. When he was ten, he had overheard his parents talking about him when they thought he was asleep. "I wonder whom he takes after," his father had said. "He hasn't got the family chin, isn't that odd?"

The young boy looked at himself in the mirror the next day. He never noticed his chin before, but now it looked terrible to him. How had he overlooked the way it receded?

He went to the family album and looked at pictures of his family—uncles, grandfather, cousins. "Strong faces, especially the men," he thought. "Not one receding chin! I'm the only one!"

Unfortunately, he did not tell his parents he had overheard them, and he did not seek help for his torment. At the age of ten, considering himself an outcast, he kept his concept of his weak chin to himself, as his own personal sorrow.

As he grew into adolescence, his sensitivity about his chin grew and grew. He was afraid to show his profile to people so he would face them directly. This got him into ridiculous situations in which he would constantly move about to prevent the offending profile from showing. People began to notice how nervous he was and laughed at his eccentricity. Finally, he told his parents how bitter he was about his chin, and they took him to see me.

Luckily, I was able to help him. I told him that objectively his chin was not a bad one at all, that his "truth" about himself was pure fiction. Not only that, I told him that he was no weakling, that he had to realize that he was as good as anyone else. I enlisted the help of his parents. His father had, of course, long since forgotten that he had ever made the remark—and he had made it casually and innocently at the time. They both assured him that he was a fine-looking young man and that his chin, while not the typical family chin, was reasonably normal.

Naturally, a concept which one has held of oneself for eight years doesn't go away in a day. But after several weeks, with his parents helping him to see the real truth, he began to feel more at peace with himself.

Slowly, his truth about himself changed. He went to college and, along with his rising self-esteem, he became a wonderful student. He majored in languages, became a successful writer, got married, had children, and today he doesn't waste his time worrying about an absurd, untruthful idea.

People's actions always depend on what they think is true about themselves and their environment. This is fundamental; it is the way we are built. We act as if our concepts are valid, no matter how misguided they are.

Experiments with hypnotism also illustrate this point.

Don Newcomb, at one point in his brilliant baseball career, was afraid to travel on planes. The big pitcher thought he knew the truth: that an airplane he boarded would crash.

Newcomb went to see a hypnotist. He was told, under hypnosis, that his plane would not crash, and the practitioner bought round-trip plane tickets for himself and Newcomb— New York to Detroit and back. Apparently really convinced of this new truth, Don relaxed on the plane and enjoyed the trip.

Los Angeles Dodger shortstop Maury Wills was also helped by hypnotism. An electrifying base-stealer, Wills at one time began to worry about his legs. He thought that they pained him, but there was no cause for the pain.

The hypnotist, putting him in a trance, said that it would be too bad if his worry undermined his base-stealing ability. To Wills' amazement, his pain vanished. In an indirect way, the hypnotist had told him the truth about his legs and he had accepted it.

People under hypnosis have taken action on the most unlikely truths. Told that water is champagne, they have become intoxicated. Informed that the weather is warm, they have perspired; then told that it is cold (same situation, same temperature), they have shivered and put on additional clothing.

Told he was Frank Sinatra, a hypnotic subject reached for a nonexistent microphone and began singing until the hypnotist told him a new "truth" to which he quickly adjusted.

These people, under hypnosis, accepted new truths—some false, some true. But enough of them! How about yourself? What is your truth about yourself?

Do you undervalue yourself? Most people do. Is your truth about yourself that you're too thin or that your nose is too long or that you're stupid, or that you'll never succeed at anything, or that you have bad luck? Not only are these "truths" negative, they are also false. You must remember that God created you for a purpose: to do good on this earth for yourself and your fellow men. You must remember that each of you, no matter how painful your past experiences, has something unique and positive in him. You must understand that each of you, no matter how downtrodden, has something good to offer.

Too many of you hypnotize—and that is not too strong a word—yourself with false beliefs about yourself. You are your own worst enemy; you undermine yourself with critical "truths" that even your actual real enemy wouldn't think. You base feelings of inferiority on evidence that any fair-minded jury would reject. Your "truth" is not truth at all; it is often just a prejudiced case directed against yourself— one more unkind than you would level against any of your acquaintances. You give yourself as much justice as would a lynch mob.

You Are Unique

God did not mass-produce the human race; people do not roll off an assembly line uniformly like the latest model automobile. He made people of different shapes and sizes, and of different skin color. He created people with many more subtle distinctions. He made each of us unique and individual —and He didn't set up standards to which we must conform.

You are unique; this is an obvious truth. You should see this fact as a positive life force, not as a fact to substantiate a feeling that you're inferior.

Yet most people mar their lives with inferiority feelings, and thus put obstacles between them and success and happiness.

Every person on earth is in some way inferior to some other person. Certainly I cannot hit a golf ball as far as Arnold Palmer. I cannot dance as well as Fred Astaire. For that matter, I cannot equal Cassius Clay in either boxing or showmanship. Acknowledging these lacks does not make me feel inferior—not in the slightest. I do not compare myself to them; I accept myself just as I am. Every day I meet people—bookkeepers, salesmen, corporation presidents—who are superior to me in some area. So what? These people cannot improve a scarred face, and there are other things I

17

can do better than they can. And they have no cause to feel inferior to me for these reasons.

When we feel inferior, it is because we measure ourselves against somebody else and convince ourselves of the entirely ridiculous idea that we should be like "somebody else" or even "everybody else." Certainly this is a false conception, for "everybody else" is made up of individuals, no two of whom are the same.

We stack evidence against ourselves, and this evidence is often based on false premises.

Many people, in their cruelty to themselves, believe that they are so inferior that they simply cannot live with themselves. To make life tolerable, they then strive to be superior. They then drive and drive themselves, making themselves thoroughly miserable in their enslavement in a web of untruth.

Inferiority and superiority are merely opposite sides of the same coin—and the cure lies in simply understanding that the coin itself is counterfeit.

For the simple truth is that you are neither "inferior" nor "superior" to your fellow human beings.

"You" are "you" and that's the whole story!

The truth is that, as a personality, you are not in competition with anyone else. God made you a unique individual. You will never be the same as another person and you were never meant to be.

This is not something phony, something sugar-coated to make you feel better. *This is the real truth.* It is your negative "truth" which is false.

Thinking Can Make It So

You might be thinking, "This is all well and good. But my 'truths' about myself are negative and they've been that way for a long time. Can I change them?"

Yes, you can. Think new thoughts about yourself! See yourself in a new light, as an individual like no one else on earth! Forget your past failures, bury them, and think of your successes, no matter how few. Remember that you have an obligation to yourself to make your life on this earth as happy as possible.

Believe in this new truth, and act on it! Resolve to be your own friend, not your enemy!

I'm not telling you that it's easy to change your basic truths but if you keep at it, following the suggestions I will outline in this book, applying yourself to the practice exercises, I assure you that you can do it. In doing so, you change the self-image with which you rise and fall.

How to Turn "As If" into Reality

Your second item of equipment is functional and creative, and will help you most to develop a true and successful self-image. It is your imagination.

Imagination is as elusive as joy or sorrow. You can't put it in a bottle or get it out of one. It has no shape, and yet it gives you shape.

Imagination is what puts the "I" in "Image." It enters into our every act. It is imagination which gives us the goal for which we head. We act or fail to act; our acts are accelerated or frozen because of imagination.

If you use your imagination positively, you can make yourself a bigger person.

In the Stanislavski school of method acting, we find a wonderful example of imagination put to use. A method actor playing a king in a Shakespearean drama tries to think *as if* he were that king. He tries to put himself completely into this king's shoes. He stands on the stage and projects this *as if* into a living reality for the audience.

Actors, in general, are able to do this. One day last year, I visited an acting school, where a director's class was scheduled. I joined a group of people who were standing around informally, watching a scene the director had mapped out for two young people, one a well-known actress. In this play, the girl was acting the part of a 16th or 17th century girl who was accused of witchcraft. When she imagined she was this girl, she acted the part so well that when on trial, being accused, looking up angrily at the heavens, she seemed to me the very force of evil. You could understand how unenlightened, superstitious people in those days could believe in something so absurd (in reality) as witchcraft.

Some actors, using their imaginations, are able to completely change the images they project. Dick Powell changed from song-and-dance man to tough-guy detective and was successful as both. James Cagney has been equally convincing as "the good guy," the vicious killer, or an eccentric ship's captain. June Allyson, after many years of being the sweet, wholesome girl, played the shrewd manipulator and was believable.

There are actors who can change their self-image with such skill that when you see them on the screen it is hard to even recognize their face as the same one you've seen in other motion pictures. I think this is the case with Geraldine Page, whose drug-addicted actress in the moving picture "Sweet Bird of Youth" seemed completely unrelated to her bashful spinster in "Summer and Smoke."

But the use of imagination is not limited to the actor, or to other creative artists.

You use it as they do—every day.

Are you worried? You are using your imagination—seeing yourself and what can happen to you.

Worry is a state of mind—before the event happens.

Do You Worry about Things That Never Happen?

Too many of us use our imaginations negatively; we worry. Not that worry doesn't sometimes have a positive function; it can prevent catastrophes, even save our very lives. But many people worry destructively. They stop up their creative energies, keep themselves from relaxing and continually imagine things that never happen.

There's one man I know, a businessman, whose father smoked a lot and five years ago died of cancer of the throat. Ever since his father's death, this man has worried about cancer. First he stopped smoking, but this did not stop the torrent of anxiety. At the first sign of a cold—or even a husky voice—he rushed to see the doctor. He thought about cancer all the time. When he read articles in newspapers and magazines about cancer, his worries increased and he read less. Eventually his imaginings dominated his life and, deciding he'd had enough worry, he retired from his lifework, thinking that might help him relax. He still worries, though, and his health is still fine.

A woman, a former patient of mine, has an imagination which tortures her every day of her life. Instead of one worry, she has many. She fears heart attacks, nuclear holocausts, stock market catastrophes, deaths of dear ones, and devotes her God-given gift of imagination to negative ends.

Now, of course, unpleasant things do happen now and then. I don't mean the "never" to be taken literally. But people like this who worry constantly imagine things that, to be exact, *rarely* happen. And their worry is more apt to do harm than good!

You Can Get That Pay Raise from the Boss

Let's take a common situation and see how you can use your imagination—positively or negatively—and what the results will be in each case.

You work in an office. You've held down the same job for two years and you want a raise in pay. You're entitled to more money, you feel, since you've done good work. You have another child and you need the money.

But you feel discouraged when you imagine what the boss' reaction will be. You picture the approaching interview in your mind. You'll knock timidly on his door—you always were afraid of the boss—and enter his private office. He'll be talking on the phone and signing letters at the same time and you'll sit down and wait for him to finish his phone call. You'll fidget in your chair and wonder if it's really such a good idea to ask for a raise—you could wait another six months, couldn't you?—and, after all, he is such a busy man. You worry about what you should say first. Perhaps he'd be annoyed if you asked for a raise too directly. Maybe you should start talking about some neutral subject like the weather or . . .

All right, do you think you'll get the raise? I doubt it. Your imagination has betrayed you. You see yourself a failure. And so you'll probably fail.

Now, let's put imagination to use again, but this time on your side.

21

Once again, mentally picture the situation. You'll knock on the boss' door. You won't smash it in, but won't feel timid about it because you're asking for a raise that you know you deserve. You'll walk up to his desk, stride crisply and confidently, and sit down, waiting for him to finish his phone call. When he finishes, you'll ask him for your raise, knowing full well that you're worth every nickel you're asking for, and knowing that the boss realizes that too. You are confident that you'll achieve what you're aiming at—your pay raise!

Do you think you'll get it now? I do, because you are using your imagination to enhance your self-image. Put simply, *you are betting on yourself!*

I know men who have used their imagination to see opportunities where other people saw nothing. There's one fellow —and he wasn't well educated, in terms of college degrees— who 25 or 30 years ago bought some small brownstone houses in an undeveloped area about a half mile from Central Park in New York City. He was not a wealthy man, but he saved his money and bought this property.

People laughed at him, called him an idiot. But he was the bright one actually; he had vision. He saw that a day was coming when this area—not too far from the huge park —had to improve. Today he is a millionaire and people call him a genius in business. In truth, this man had confidence in his imagination.

If I am a well-known plastic surgeon today, it is because I used my imagination and set goals for myself. When I started my medical training over 30 years ago and told people I was interested in plastic surgery, they scoffed. At the time it was a little-publicized field. "Where can you study?" they asked.

My mother wept. She wanted me to be a general practitioner, become assistant to our family doctor, work up a safe, sure practice.

But I had this vision and I imagined ways in which I could help others as a plastic surgeon, how I could give people new faces which would help them feel better about themselves. I assured my mother that I knew what I was doing, and I made it my business to reach my goals.

I studied with men in Paris, Berlin, Vienna, London, who

had done plastic surgery during World War I. Then I came back home and opened my office. Everyone predicted failure.

But my imagination told me that people would need a good plastic surgeon and I was right. The first month was difficult, but then my practice started growing.

Putting a Smile on Your Self-Image

"How about me?" you may ask. "What can I do?"

You can do plenty. I'm going to show you how to use your imagination as your friend, to improve your self-image and give you new life. I say "new" because too many of us have given up on life; our imaginations have let us down.

Napoleon Bonaparte once wrote, "The human race is governed by its imagination."

But to many people, unfortunately, imagination is not good government. It is a breeder of death and failure. ". . . but the Imagination is conscious of an indestructible dominion," wrote the great English poet William Wordsworth.

True, but will your imagination's dominion lead you to success or failure, to happiness or misery? In these pages you will learn to use more imagination as a tool for happiness, a constructor of a healthy self-image.

Our recent realization that our behavior stems from our images and beliefs gives us a new, potent weapon in changing personality. It opens up a new door leading to the good life.

For you act and feel according to the image your mind holds of what things are like, which might be quite different from reality. Moreover, if our mental images of ourselves are twisted, our reaction to our surroundings will be doubly unrealistic.

If we picture ourselves functioning in specific situations, it is nearly the same as the actual performance. Mental practice helps one to perform better in real life.

A psychologist, using controlled experimental conditions, found that mental practice could help people throw darts accurately. His subjects sat each day in front of the target imagining they were throwing darts at it; it improved their aim as much as actually throwing the darts.

Golfers use this technique. When you next watch a golf

tournament on TV note how the pro rehearses his shot, imagines what is going to happen, before he actually strokes the ball.

Shadowboxing is a classical example of people using their imagination to prepare them for a successful experience in the prize ring.

How can this help you? You can "shadowbox" in the areas that are meaningful to you. I gave you an example of mental picturing when I discussed getting the pay raise from the boss. The fellow who probably got the raise saw himself as smiling and efficient, and imagined his boss responding to the integrity of his self-image.

This can work for you; you can become a more positive person. You can image the self you'd like to be and see yourself in new roles. You can change your personality, become more whole than you've ever been, if you build a stronger self-image.

Let's get one thing straight, though. The aim of self-image psychology is not to create a fictitious self which is omnipotent. Such an image is as untrue as the inferior image of oneself. Our aim is to find the best we have in us, realistically, and to bring it out into the open. Why should you continue to short-change yourself?

Your Success Mechanism

Your imagination is so important because it can trigger off your success mechanism, the great creative mechanism within you which can implement your success in life. I described this mechanism at great length in *Psycho-Cybernetics*, which you should read if you want a complete technical understanding of it.

The science of cybernetics has led us to the understanding that your so-called "subconscious mind" is not a "mind" but a goal-striving servo-mechanism consisting of the brain and nervous system which the mind directs. We do not have two "minds," but a mind or consciousness which operates an automatic, goal-oriented machine. Basically, this machine functions like an electronic servo-mechanism but it is more wonderful than any man-made electronic brain.

This inner mechanism is impersonal. It will work automatically to achieve the goals which you yourself set for it. Feed it "success goals" and it functions as a "success mechanism." Feed it negative aims and it operates as a "failure mechanism."

Like any servo-mechanism, it must have a clearly defined objective toward which to work.

Our automatic mechanism seeks to reach objectives presented in the form of mental pictures, which we create by using our imagination.

The main goal-image is our self-image, which defines the limits of our endeavors, the areas in which we must operate.

Our creative mechanism works on the data we feed it, just like any other servo-mechanism. Our thoughts are funneled into it, describing the problem which it must tackle. In this sense, our beliefs and our mental pictures predetermine the final results.

If we provide our automatic mechanism with information about our inferiority, a reflection of a poor self-image, it will process this data, working as a "failure mechanism," translating this into objective experience. Too many of us do this.

To accelerate your determination to get more out of life, you must learn to use your great creative mechanism as a success mechanism, not as a failure mechanism. You must develop new ways of thinking and imaging to that you will build a strong, reality-oriented self-image, which will give nourishment to your success mechanism, leading the way to happiness.

In the practice exercise in this chapter, and in succeeding chapters, I will show you how to use your imagination to put a smile on your self-image and a spring in your stride and a song in your soul. I will show you how to picture your past successes—not your failures—and carry this successful self-image forward into the operational success that constitutes the good life.

Practice Exercise No. 1: Building a New Self-Image

You formed your present self-image from mental pictures of yourself in the past, growing out of judgments you placed on your experiences in life. We will now work on building a healthy self-image with this same use of imagery.

But first, remember this: Change will not come without effort! You must work hard to realize inspiring results.

You must be willing to set aside time daily for this exercise, as well as for the other practice exercises in this book. I would suggest an hour a day. Don't make yourself a slave to this schedule but discipline yourself so that nine days out of ten you're working on these exercises—until you get the results you want. If improving your self-image is important to you—and it should be—you'll find the time.

Sit down or lie down somewhere that is restful and quiet. Relax and make yourself as comfortable as you can. Then close your eyes and let your God-given imagination work for you.

In the theater of your mind, picture yourself as you truly like yourself. Imagine that you are looking at a motion picture screen, watching a picture of yourself. See yourself, in a problem situation, as you've been in your best moments handling this situation. I can't tell you specifically what areas to focus on—this is individual. But I can give you a fictitious example, and you can take it from there.

Suppose you're a young woman, 22, single, and you've quit your steno job because you didn't like it. You want a job as a private secretary and you know you'll be good at it.

Your trouble is that job interviews make you nervous and inhibited. Every time you've ever looked for a job, your self-image has been weak.

No, that's not true. There was once, when you were 16, and you wanted a job as swimming counselor at a girls' summer camp. You felt *good* that day. Fine! Picture that interview, *seeing and feeling every detail in your imagination.*

You walked into the office building, high heels click-clacking in the lobby. The camp's office was on the 13th floor and you laughed at their lack of superstition. You smiled at the elevator operator and he said. "Good morning!"

The camp's office was one small room, but you didn't feel cramped. You sat down and smoothed your dress. You were wearing your black dress with gold buttons, and your hair sparkled. You felt pretty and you weren't worried about the interview—you felt too good for that. The interviewer, sitting in a leather swivel chair, seemed friendly to you because you felt friendly.

Keep visualizing this scene in detail, feeling once again the confidence you felt during this interview. See everything in your mind—the mahogany desk, the interviewer's eyeglasses —until this past success is part of you and you are ready to act on it, forgetting your fear of other interviews, making this new confidence part of a growing self-image.

I created this example in my imagination just to show you generally what I mean. Now apply this potent method to your own realistic case.

Perhaps you're a man in your sixties. You no longer work and devote much of your time to community activities. You enjoy belonging to organizations but when there's a public discussion, you can't seem to talk as you'd like to. You crawl into a shell instead, fearful of being the center of attention. Still, there was that time ten years ago . . .

Perhaps you're a younger man, in your thirties, the family breadwinner, and you love to play tennis but feel self-conscious and awkward when you get out on the court. Still, how about that time you beat Frank, the only time you ever beat him? . . .

Maybe you're a woman in your fifties. Your children have grown up and married and, when you see them, you feel like a stranger to them, unable to relate meaningfully to their world, unable to meet them halfway. Still, how about the warm, sincere talk you had six months ago with your daughter-in-law before you both put your defenses back up? . . .

Only you know what your problem situations are; you feel them in your heart. During this practice period, focus on a basic problem situation, with this important switch: *This time you are seeing yourself, in the theater of your mind, handling this situation as you would like to handle it.* This time you are successful and you bring this success back onto your inner motion picture screen and see it again and again.

During this extremely vital practice period, see yourself over and over acting and reacting the way you would like to in a difficult situation, activating your success mechanism. How you acted yesterday doesn't matter; how you act tomorrow doesn't matter. See yourself as a success; keep this image alive. Imagine your feelings if you were to become the kind of person you'd like to be, in terms of your real potentialities. If certain situations have frightened you, picture yourself mastering them, winning out over your inhibitions, slaying the dragon of failure.

The power of your imagination is so tremendous that it may take you weeks to realize it. For a while you may doubt this great power because it is intangible, you cannot touch it. But Jesus Christ's message was intangible; so are the beliefs of most religious and political philosophers. Faith itself is one of our greatest possessions, and it is not material.

As time goes on and you continue to use your imagination positively, funneling information into your success mechanism, you may be surprised to find that your new picture of yourself is becoming a reality. You are going out into the world with more confidence, you are acting differently. Your image of yourself is getting stronger with each passing day.

3

The Secret Strength
in Relaxation

"Ah, what is more blessed than to put care aside, when the mind lays down its burden, and spent with distant travel, we come home again and rest on the couch we longed for?" So wrote Catullus, the great Roman poet, several thousand years ago.

But so few of us rest these days. Relaxation seems to be a lost art. Is it the hustle and bustle of modern civilization, the frenzied pace of scientific discovery, are these too much for mere human beings?

Doubtless modern conditions are not ideal, but consider this: God made each of us to enjoy life, not to bury it in countless anxieties. He meant us to savor His world in calmness, not to rush around it in perplexed consternation.

Many call these times "the age of anxiety." Some people even accept worry, insomnia, stomach ulcers as the price for living in today's world.

But it does not have to be like this, and in this chapter I'll give you some ideas on how to relax and be at peace with yourself—whether you are watching a peaceful pastoral scene or working in a crowded office. At the end of this chapter you will find a practice exercise aimed at helping you relax; I will show you how to achieve calm, no matter what your circumstances.

Easy Does It!

People today try too hard, push themselves too hard. They frantically drive themselves in their struggle to make money, become beautiful, or overcome their inferiority feelings. Too often the end does not justify the means; certainly material wealth cannot compensate for the loss of one's good health.

We see so many obviously anxious, driven people every day. Others seem relaxed, but are merely masters of the art of concealment.

What price material success? Is it worth hypertension? Is it worth the sacrifice of one's health?

Millions of people today suffer from excess tension, a disease more common than the so-called common cold. It is the rare person who is calm. In one way or another, hypertension probably afflicts more people and is more destructive than all the diseases we lie awake worrying about, such as cancer and cardiac trouble.

But just as tension can make you sick, relaxation can make you well.

Medical authorities have cited relaxation as an aid to sufferers of heart trouble. They have prescribed relaxation as a relief—even a cure—for people in high-pressure occupations who have heart trouble.

Researchers in the field of psychosomatic medicine have documented the close connection between emotional and physical health.

In writing this book, however, I am not primarily interested in physical disease. Basically, I want to show you how to be good to yourself, how to change your self-image and enjoy life more. And, in this chapter, I want you to learn how to relax.

Why don't you start right now? If you're sitting in an armchair, nervously tapping your feet, a frown on your forehead, relax, settle down, stop worrying, while I tell you a story about a man I've known for many years.

He's a businessman, and he's made a fortune. He's earned millions, and he's saved quite a bit too. But—and I've seen him hundreds of times—he never seems relaxed.

Relax in the playhouse of your mind and watch the scene

as I unfold it for you. See it before you—see it with your own eyes!

He's just come home from work and he's just stepped into his dining room. The furniture is a rich mahogany, a long table and six chairs, but he doesn't notice it. He sits down at the table, but he's restless, so he paces around the room. He bangs the table absent-mindedly and almost trips over a chair. His wife sits down; he says hello and drums the table until a servant brings in the food. He gobbles the food down as fast as he can, as if his hands were two shovels hurling it down a hole.

Dinner over, he gets up quickly and walks into the living-room. It's a decorative room, with a long, beautiful sofa and plush, upholstered chairs, wall-to-wall carpeting and rich paintings. He hurls himself into a chair, picking up a news-paper in almost the same motion. He ruffles a few pages, scans the headlines, throws it to the ground, picks up a cigar. He bites off the tip of the cigar, lights it, puffs twice and puts it out in the ashtray.

He just can't find himself. But suddenly he springs up, goes to the television set and turns it on. As the picture comes to life, he turns it off impatiently. He strides to the hall closet, grabs his hat and coat, and goes out for a walk.

This man has done this hundreds of times. I know, I've seen him do it. With all his successes, he has not learned to relax. He is a dynamo of tension, bringing home from his office the spasms of his occupation.

He has no economic problems, his home is an interior decorator's dream, he owns two cars, his servants attend to his every command—but he cannot relax. Not only that, he has even forgotten who he is. In his drive toward success and prestige, he's given all his time to achieve material success, and in the process of making money, he's undone himself.

Suppose we bring him back onto the stage of your mind so that a friend can question him. This friend wants to help him to relax and become himself. The conversation goes like this:

Friend: Who are you?
    He: You know who I am. I'm Mr. X.

Friend: Is that all you are? Just a name?

He: Are you crazy? I'm head of Y Corporation. Why, I'm the head of the whole industry.

Friend: Yes, I know, but you're a failure in a much more important industry, in your own personal industry, in the greatest industry in the world. You've forgotten who you are. You're made up of assets and liabilities.

He: What! Don't you think I know that?

Friend: You don't understand. I'm talking about other liabilities—not business. About your status as a human being. You have no dignity, no understanding, no sympathy for yourself. You've got research to improve your business product, but how about improving your personal product— yourself? Is money everything? Or is self-direction important too? How about some compassion for yourself, for your self-image? Give it the relaxation it needs. How about accepting yourself as you are instead of always outdoing the Joneses?

He: I think well of myself. I—

Friend: No, you don't. You like yourself as a businessman, not as a person. When you're not working, you don't know what to do with yourself. Don't outdo the Joneses, just keep up with yourself. Find yourself. Then you'll be able to sit still and relax, find out who you are, work at improving yourself.

All right, you, sitting in the playhouse of your mind, maybe the friend helped this man. Maybe his advice has inspired him, put him on the road to relaxation. But how about helping yourself? Can you help yourself to relax?

But do I hear you say, "He has position and money, while I have none"?

This doesn't matter. You, too, can relax if you just do the best you can and then accept yourself realistically, as you are, with your limitations. Stop punishing yourself! Have compassion for yourself! See your strengths as well as your weaknesses. *See yourself as you are, a human being with unique, individual qualities. Relax with your image of your self and, as you relax, others will relax with you and appreciate you more and more.*

When you're grappling with a problem, do your best, your very best. If you achieve your goal, wonderful! If you don't, and you've already done your best, give yourself a little common-sense advice: that you can do no more. Take a walk, go to a movie, go to sleep—in short, let go, give up all conscious responsibility for the outcome.

You will be surprised how, often, the answer you've been struggling for will come to you out of nowhere while you're doing some menial task or thinking about something entirely different.

Surely an intelligent person should set his goals, gather his information, arrange his materials and work earnestly and efficiently. I'm not telling you that magic will come to your aid. But when you've reached your limit and everything still isn't just the way you'd like it, learn to take it easy. Learn to relax and treat yourself just as if you were a human being put on this planet to enjoy life. Your imagination surely needs a rest now and then if it's to function as a friend.

Let Bygones Be Bygones!

"And their sins should be forgiven them" (Mark iv: 12). "Father, forgive them, for they know not what they do" (Luke xxiii: 34).

These quotes from the Bible point up the great importance of forgiveness—of yourself as well as of others. You cannot relax and be at peace with yourself if you carry grudges around with you. If your job was to unload heavy crates of oranges from a truck and carry them into a supermarket, wouldn't you feel overburdened if you had to lift up a crate on your shoulders instead and carry it around with you all day? Could you relax? Of course not. Well, you cannot relax and carry grudges around with you all day long either. The two just don't go together.

There are many fallacies about forgiveness, and one reason that its therapeutic value has not received full recognition is that *real* forgiveness has been so rare. We have been told that we are "good" if we forgive, but have seldom been advised that the act of forgiveness can relax us, can reduce our load of hostility.

Another idea is that forgiving places us in a strategic position, is a means of winning out over our foes. This is a way of saying that forgiveness can be used as an effective weapon of revenge—and it can be. But revengeful forgiveness is not real.

Real forgiveness is not difficult—it's much easier than holding a grudge. There is only one essential condition. You must be willing to give up your sense of condemnation; you must cancel out the debt, with no mental reservations.

When we find it hard to forgive, it is because we enjoy our sense of condemnation. We get a morbid satisfaction from it. As long as we can condemn another, we can feel superior to him.

In nursing a grudge, many people also derive a perverse sense of satisfaction in feeling sorry for themselves. When we really forgive, we are not doing someone a favor or showing off our righteousness. We cancel out the debt not because we have made the other person pay long enough for the harm he has done us, but because we have come to see that the debt itself is not valid. True forgiveness comes only when we are able to see that there is and was nothing for us to forgive. We should not have condemned the other person in the first place.

But the main point is that if you want to relax, to enjoy peace of mind, you must learn to bury grudges. You must become a forgiving person. Be a lover, not a hater. In the words of the great French writer, La Rochefoucauld, "One pardons in the degree that one loves."

The Secret of Living with Yourself

As human beings we all live with, or near, other people and must learn to live in harmony with them. We must learn to compromise, to give and take, to shine in the spotlight and yet surrender it gracefully.

Learning to live with people and machines, with changing

customs and the threat of nuclear war, all this is not easy. But the most important secret of all is learning to live with yourself. If you can learn to do that, you'll get along somehow—no matter what is going on around you. And you'll be able to relax.

In his essay "Self-Reliance," Ralph Waldo Emerson wrote:

"There is a time in every man's education when he arrives at the conviction that envy is ignorance, that imitation is suicide, that he must take himself for better or worse as his portion; that though the wide universe is full of good, no kernel of nourishing corn can come to him but through the toil bestowed on that plot of ground which is given to him to till. The power which resides in him is new in nature, and none but he knows what that is which he can do, nor does he know until he has tried. . . . Trust thyself: every heart vibrates to that iron string."

We can learn much from his message today. We have made scientific discoveries in the past 20 or 30 years that stagger the imagination. Technologically, we are an amazing people. The cleverness of our minds seems to know no limits when it comes to grappling with mechanical problems. Haven't you ever marveled at our astronautical accomplishments at Cape Canaveral? I know that I am sometimes astounded at New York's skyscrapers, which I see every day. Once in a while I wonder how they were so well made of steel and concrete, so perfectly planned, that you never hear of one of them falling down.

And yet we have not learned to live with other human beings and relax!

Moreover, most people today cannot be alone—for even a short period of time—and find it tolerable.

It's no accident that a New York radio station told listeners that they'd never be alone while tuning in its programs, feeling that this would be a comforting statement to many people.

David Riesman, in his popular book *The Lonely Crowd,* (Yale University Press, 1950) stresses modern man's fear of being alone. ". . . What is it that drives men who have been surrounded with people and their problems on the day shift to see often the same company on the night shift. Perhaps in part it is the terror of loneliness . . .

". . . When I asked young people in interviews how they would feel if for some reason the radio should be shut off, quite a few were frightened at the prospect. . . . One veteran of the Pacific campaign, who had spent two years in Korea, said he had once been at a summer place in Wisconsin where for two weeks there was no radio. He said he couldn't stand it; nothing in the army where he had the Armed Forces Network, was so bad. Without the noise of the radio, it seems, people feel as if their own receptors are dead. And indeed they have used the noise of others to deaden the noise of the self."

I've met many people to whom a day—even a few hours—alone is sheer torture. One comes to mind right away. He was a good salesman, a "jolly good fellow" type, he could sell anything to anybody, but he never sold himself on *himself*. His eye was always on business. When he went to play golf, there was no enjoyment in it; he was just after business deals with his partners. He never found release or relaxation and dreaded being alone; he would go to any lengths to avoid solitude, even if it meant buying people supper or drinks or entertaining them with an endless repertoire of anecdotes.

This poor fellow died of a heart attack in his forties and I doubt that he ever enjoyed one good, sincere talk with himself during his lifetime.

I'm sure that many of you find it most difficult to be alone. At the first hint of peace and quiet, you panic and head urgently for the radio or television set, to be soothed by the thunder of horses' hooves as the "good guys" chase the "bad guys" through western prairies that look mighty familiar by now.

This is a far cry from the days of Henry David Thoreau. In *Walden* he wrote that ". . . I went to the woods because I wished to live deliberately, to front only the essential facts of life, and see if I could not learn what it had to teach, and not, when I come to die, discover that I had not lived."

I do not advocate solitude as a way of life but at times being alone is good—in small doses. You can then return to the people around you, refreshed, to give them the best you've got in you. But, as a way of life, solitude is an evasion which defeats you. One should, however, have the capacity to find one's own company entertaining—alone or with others. One should be able to relax—alone or with others.

The whole art of relaxation is to accept yourself, to be part of your fellow men in give-and-take relationships, respecting them as human beings with faults and respecting yourself.

In learning to live with yourself, the final key must be the health of your self-image. If you see yourself realistically, giving yourself the respect you deserve, picturing your successes and your loving feelings, keeping faith with yourself in spite of your faults, forgiving yourself for your mistakes—then you have found the secret of living with yourself without fear.

How to Relax on the Job

People have to make money to live; therefore, their most realistic fears often center around their jobs. Since fear and tension are twins, it's not surprising to hear people complain that they just can't relax on the job.

One man who completed dozens of bombing missions over Germany as an Air Force pilot during World War II—with confidence—revealed to me that he feels great anxiety in his routine office job.

In *The Split-Level Trap*, by Dr. Richard E. Gordon, Katherine K. Gordon and Max Gunther (Bernard Geis Associates, 1960–1961), there are some interesting case studies of people's emotional problems, many of which center around their vocations.

One man returned from World War II to a lucrative selling job. He moved with his wife and three children to a larger, more expensive apartment and filled it with furniture bought on credit. Shortly after, his job vanished when his company merged with another organization. He was told he could quit or take a job at lower pay in the parent company's sales office. He took the job.

His drive to succeed was strong. With real economic pressures pushing him, he drove himself ruthlessly, paid off his debts, and became a star salesman. When a minor executive position was offered him, he was not ready for it but felt he could not refuse.

By now he had bought a house in the suburbs, along with a new load of furniture and appliances, and a new car. He began to assume an air of confidence to fit in with his status. His wife, striving for social acceptance in the community, gave expensive cocktail parties and joined the country club.

He could not relax. "The drive to get ahead had come to dominate him, and anything that did not contribute to that goal was an irritation. A day's adventure with a boy (his son), a quiet afternoon in the shade of a tree, a good book, a symphony, these things lose their magic when the mind is too strongly preoccupied with material striving. . . . Relaxation comes in well-practiced activities that are not associated with danger, punishment, fear or strain." He developed an ulcer.

He began to feel pinned down to one job in one company because, realistically, all his eggs were in one basket. He knew of no other economic areas he could turn to if he failed in this job. He became more and more tense on the job.

Finally, he began to see how diversity could improve his position. He began to chat with people about job possibilities in other companies. He found job areas in these companies where he might fit in. This reduced his fear of failure in his own job and set off a series of dynamic improvements in his personal life and that of his family.

This study, which has profound sociological implications, offers one very practical suggestion on how to relax on the job: *diversify*. Be as independent of your boss and your company as you can, so you realistically need fear nothing.

This is an uncertain, changing world, and the more possible sources of income you have, the more you can objectively afford to relax. The other day I hailed a taxi and struck up a conversation with the taxi driver. He told me he'd been hacking just two months; for years he'd owned a butcher shop with a partner in the Bronx. They had made good money for a long time, but now incoming supermarkets were taking the profit out of their formerly thriving business. He had not foreseen this happening and felt depressed for months. Finally, being a resourceful man, he turned to driving a taxi part time and was making fairly good money at it. With a second source of income available, he was no longer worried about his declining butcher trade.

Try not to carry grudges on the job. Don't be resentful of the guy making more money than you do, don't hate the boss because he can give you orders!

The best way I know how to relax on the job is to do the best you can every day and allow this to give you content- ment. Perhaps you can get a better job someday, but in the meanwhile feel proud of your daily performance and see yourself as you are—someone who does his best, and who has every right to relax in this knowledge.

You Can Help Others Ease Their Tension

The great joy of relaxation is that it's contagious. If you are at peace with yourself, you can spread relaxation to others—and happiness too. Relaxation is the first stage of happiness.

I know an amazing man with great inner wealth. His eyes are calm and friendly and he has a warm smile for every- body he meets. He helps others ease their tension—far better than tranquilizers—because he is full of peace and love.

Every week he goes to a certain hospital to visit the patients, many of whom are tense, uncertain of the future. He sits with them for 20 or 30 minutes, listens to their worries and calms their fears. They are strangers to him, yet he goes to cheer them up.

He does not expect a reward; this is his nature, to sit with people and chat, to be cordial and concerned.

Many times he has painted the day in bright colors for some suffering human being. How wonderful it would be if his relaxation could spread like an infectious disease, bathing the world in his kindness!

Don't Drive Yourself!

A few years ago a friend said to me, "I like my work, I love my family, I've had a good life and I can go home and relax. I think I'm a lucky man. But when I get in a car and get out on the highway and head for the city, I get tense all over and it takes me a few hours before I can shake off this feeling of tension."

My reaction was immediate. "Don't drive!" I told him. "You don't have to. You can take the train in to work. If you're not relaxed when you drive, it's doing you harm."

He took my advice and today his life is more restful.

I'm not concerned with driving here—it tenses up some people and relaxes others—but with the avoidance of *driving yourself.*

Too many people force themselves to do things because they feel others expect it of them. Most adults drive a car today so my friend, a successful man in many ways, felt that he had to drive—even though he hated it.

You cannot relax and force yourself; the two don't go together. While there are some things in life that you are compelled to do, you often have a free choice which you do not exercise. As individuals, we must choose the kind of life that is good for us.

You Can Only Do So Much

Unfortunately, we often are our worst enemies. Many people just keep on driving and driving, pushing themselves harder than even a Scrooge-type employer would. They may rationalize their on-the-go life, stating that they're trying to make money or to get something out of life, but they're really just destroying themselves. Often, they're also undermining what they consider their objectives to be. Moreover, they are blurring the outlines of their self-image.

To relax, you must know what your limits are, know when it's time to pack in the work and play a little. If your responsibilities are demanding, you must know when to seek release and how to find it.

You must understand that you are just a human being, not a whole organization or an army, and that there is just so much you can do. Don't expect the impossible of yourself!

Sometimes circumstances force people to perform beyond their limits, for a time anyway, making them tense and resentful. At times like this, it is better to explode, to let the anger burst out into the open like water pouring out of a dam. Keeping it locked inside poisons the system, makes relaxation unattainable.

You Can't Push Yourself into Sleep

Sleep is our moment of supreme relaxation, the time when we should forget all our problems, forgive all whom we think have wronged us, accept all our limitations.

> Dreams who loves dreams, forget all grief;
> Find in sleep's nothingness relief.
> —Lionel Johnson

Yes, sleep should bring us relief. It should refresh us, give us strength for the demanding day ahead of us.

But to many of us it is something else to worry about. It is a challenge, something we must accomplish. Millions of Americans take to bed each night, grimly muttering to themselves, "Sleep! I *will* go to sleep!" It's like an order, and it doesn't work. These people spend their nights tossing and turning, torturing themselves with resentful thoughts.

To sleep is to relax, and then relax some more, until waves of drowsiness steal peacefully through your body and soul, engulfing you in gentleness, until you are at peace and know no more.

Modern-day insomnia points out once again the magnitude of our real problem: our inability to relax. Sleeplessness is one of the most common symptoms of emotional distress.

Actually, the easiest way to fall asleep is to stop worrying about it. Many people, fearing they will contract illness if they don't get their quota of sleep hours, stay up into the night preventing themselves from sleeping with their fears. Yet, in lab experiments, men have stayed awake for close to

100 consecutive hours without suffering permanent ill effects. Naturally, they had trouble concentrating and were short-tempered, but just 12 hours of good sleep brought the rest-deprived man back to normal again.

So our fear of not getting enough sleep is groundless. We attack the question of sleep just as we attack other areas—hustling, bustling, pushing, trying too hard.

How easy it really is to sleep is emphasized by the sleeping customs of other cultures. The Maori of New Zealand, for example, sleep squatting on their heels with a mat tied around the neck to keep out the rain. The Japanese use a block of wood as a pillow. And you say you can't sleep on a nice, comfortable mattress with a soft pillow?

Live your day spiritedly, doing your best to achieve your goals and to live in harmony with your fellows, realistically accepting yourself, and you won't have to worry about sleep. It will just come.

First, do your work, which should take about eight hours. Then relax and enjoy yourself, leaving your work troubles where they belong—at the office or factory. Roughly, that should take about eight hours. Then you will be ready for sleep and no one will have to hint that it's getting late. You'll know it. You'll be tired, in a pleasant way, and you'll just fold up on the bed, relax with your thoughts for a while and be asleep before you know it.

When you wake up in the morning, you'll feel renewed. You'll feel energetic, ready for the day that lies ahead.

Your Self-Image and Relaxation

You must relax to be happy and I consider this area so important that I've devoted two chapters to it. Consult Chapter 14 for some more ideas that will help you find calm.

The suggestions I've already made in this chapter can be vital to your well-being. They can not only help you to live a longer life, they can also make your years more enjoyable.

I did not just jot them down on impulse; they are concepts I have formulated from my own 60-plus years of trial-and-error. They are the fruit of a lifetime of contemplation and in some cases you will be able to profit from my own mistakes.

They will aid you in living more calmly and when you're tense, I know it will help you to re-read the ideas in this chapter.

The basic idea, once again, is the health of your self-image. It cannot be otherwise because it is this picture you have of yourself which brings you success or failure and triggers off the functioning of your automatic mechanism.

You will find this theme repeated over and over in these pages because it is so basic to your happiness. I cannot write enough about it, if anything I write with understatement, because this inner quality is your one great possession in life. If you work tirelessly to change this conception of yourself, seeing yourself with ever-increasing tolerance, believing in yourself with more and more conviction, you will find the state of relaxation that you seek.

Practice Exercise No. 2: Hints to Help You Relax

As you're doing this exercise, you're once again sitting in a quiet place where you can concentrate on your thoughts, which can be amazingly effective tools.

In the last chapter, I tried to familiarize you with one of your greatest potential allies: *your imagination*. Once again we will use the fantastic power of mental picturing to help you solve your problems.

This exercise will help you when you're tensed up. Work on it now, but also go back to it any time your nerves are jangled and you feel like screaming or taking your irritation out on a friend.

Simply sit in the playhouse of your mind and envision a physical landscape which is relaxing to you.

If you like to go to the beach and stand at the ocean's edge looking out at the seemingly endless expanse of glistening water, go there—in your mind. Relax in these surroundings that you love. Recapture the full beauty of the scene in every detail; feel the sun beating down on you, hear the waves breaking against the shore, smell the refreshing, salty breeze. See the clear blue of the sky above and listen to the happy laughter of children playing at the seashore. Feel your part in Nature's plan.

If such a beach scene brings you peace, picture it over and over, feeling that you're there, relaxed, worrying about nothing. Keep imaging it until sunshine flows through you, driving the dark thoughts out. See every detail, bring the happy feeling back.

You'll be absolutely amazed at how quickly such a positive use of your imagination can help you find peace of mind.

Naturally, I'm using this beach scene as an example. You might not find a beach relaxing at all. Picture an environment that *you* love, which brings a feeling of contentment to you.

Once you feel less tense, do some concentrated thinking on two major roadblocks that keep you from relaxing.

1. *Accept your limitations*. Understand that you are just one person, and that you can do only so much. Tell yourself that you should stop driving yourself like a slave, that you should slow down. If you find yourself rushing around at a frantic pace, tell yourself to stop. Ask yourself what you're accomplishing. Would you rather drive yourself into a heart attack or relax with your human limitations? Ask yourself this question over and over, because it makes a lot of sense.

2. *Learn the healing power of forgiveness*. Tell yourself to stop holding grudges—against others *and against yourself*. You cannot afford this burden of resentment; you cannot have peace of mind while you hate. Compassion and love are parents of relaxation. If you want inner calm, make every effort to become more charitable and discard your grudges.

Now go back once again into your own inner power-house, feeling more relaxed as you do. See once again, on your own personal motion picture screen, the drama we enacted early in this chapter. Picture in your mind this pressure-driven man who cannot even relax in his own home, cannot even enjoy his dinner, cannot even sit down without jumping up and pacing the floor.

It is important that you see this man, *clearly*, the worried lines on his forehead, the fist-like clenching of his tense hands, the stiffness of his movements. Bring him to life in your mind as you see him, on the basis of my verbal description.

Bring your mental camera in for a closeup, to help yourself, because you must not just think about him, you must *see* him in your mind. For once you do, you will do everything in your power to avoid being such a personal failure as you see.

Focus on this mental image because it is the image of unhappiness, our enemy.

Now let us bring in another picture, a visualization of what we're aiming at, a model for you in your efforts to change your self-image and improve your life.

Think of a person whom your heart tells you is happy. Bring his image into the theater of your mind; see him as clearly as you can. Once more focus on his face and bring out every detail: the calm eyes, the warm smile, the relaxed facial muscles.

Mentally image him carrying on his activities and note the easy confidence with which you have seen him functioning. Feel his attitude toward problem situations and his philosophy of life. Visualize his relationships with other people, perhaps yourself, and note the friendliness with which he shakes hands and listens when you talk.

See him over and over in the theater of your mind for this is one motion picture you must not miss; this is the picture of happiness. This is the image toward which you will aim; this is the type of picture you must have stamped in your mind as you work at readjusting your picture of yourself, making yourself a relaxed, easygoing person on the road to happiness.

This is the way you want to see yourself, not just in your glass mirror but, deeper, in the mirror of your mind. When you see yourself this way, you will trigger off the success mechanism in yourself and you'll be on your way.

I must make one thing clear: You can't see yourself as exactly like this happy person whom you want to emulate. You are different people. It is the quality of happiness—this is what I want you to capture.

If you keep working on these exercises, understanding more and more the fantastic power that resides in your image of yourself, you will change your self-image. Your picture of yourself will be happier, and you will be in the process of becoming a happy person. You will be calm, knowing that you will not hurt yourself.

I wish you, my readers, a great gift: the ability to relax. If you can relax in this turbulent world of ours, you are a fortunate person—and you can be fortunate. As you read this book, absorbing the concepts and *practicing them* on the stage of your mind, you will find that you can attain a peace of mind which you never dreamed was possible.

4

Why Not Be
a Winner?

Step out on the stage of life and prepare to face the struggle, for it will be a struggle. You are one of many, and it is easy to get lost in the shuffle.

Take your mirror in your hand and apply your makeup. But, first, what is the role you will try to play? Clown—or villain? Failure—or success?

You say to me, "All my life I've seen myself as a failure."

That doesn't matter. You can succeed—if you really want to and if you're willing to work hard at it.

"But I'm no youngster," you say, "I'm not 21—or 31, either. I'm past the prime of my life. It's hard to change when you're my age."

It's true that changing may come a little harder if you're older, but the important thing is that *you still can change*. The road to success is rarely smooth. Albert Einstein, the great scientist, was actually thought a mediocre student by some of his grade-school teachers. The eminent French scientist, Louis Pasteur, was considered a failure for many years. The great movie star Clark Gable was once a time-keeping clerk at $95 a month, and later worked as a garage mechanic. Lillian Roth had to wade through years of alcoholic fog to regain stardom. Thomas Edison had such a difficult time in school that his father feared he was stupid.

Recognition did not come immediately to any of these people—and it won't for you. Probably, you'll have to set more modest goals for yourself; you must be realistic. Few scientists have the stature of an Einstein; few actors have the appeal of a Gable.

Set goals that are reasonable but, at the same time, don't underrate your potential. See yourself as you've been during your best moments.

For, even if you've failed at things most of your life, you can succeed—if you change your self-image.

See Yourself as a Success

Step out on the stage of life and look at your audience. Don't pay any attention if they jeer at you or throw tomatoes! Remember that you have a good part, the best you've ever had and you will be a success!

You may be nervous in the spotlight; don't worry about it. A little nervous energy will not harm you, will not spoil your performance, if you accept it as natural and do not let it overwhelm you.

You may miss your cues at first—you probably will. Don't let it bother you! You cannot be perfect, you never will be, and if you've been used to spending your life sitting in the audience, watching others shine, you'll have to get used to your new self-image. You'll have to break it in gently.

But these are the things to remember: *you can change, and you can succeed.* While you're sitting backstage, in the darkness, just with yourself, see yourself as the kind of person you want to be and resolve to make yourself that kind of person. Don't shoot for the moon, don't be unrealistic! If you failed high school math, you'll probably never be a physicist. But see yourself as you've been in your finest hours—no matter how fleeting—and recapture the feeling of what you *can be* in life and what you *can do.* You've got the raw material in you, each of you. Dig out your buried treasure and don't be afraid to show it to yourself and to the world.

The Meaning of Success

Success means different things to different people. To some, success and money are the same thing. To others, a good marriage and family life spell success. Some people feel successful only when engaged in the creative sense of artistic achievement.

I know one man who feels the warm glow of success when he puts through a clever business deal; it's not just the money, it's the feeling that his tactics have won out, that he's won a victory on the battlegrounds of business. He plans his deals with the imagination and careful attention to detail of a General Eisenhower planning the D-day invasion in Normandy. When his manipulations have been effective, this man feels the exhilaration, the heady wine of success.

Another acquaintance thinks of business as vulgar and greedy, a seamy side of life that one must put up with. He feels successful when he's doing something with his hands, at his country home: painting the house, plastering, building a barbecue pit.

Success is an individual thing, so you must define it for yourself. Ask yourself what it is you want to achieve, what it is that will make you feel most alive, most joyous. Forget what others would like you to think—think for yourself. You are a unique human being, like no other on earth, and only you can know your meaning of success.

Take Dead Aim on the Target!

Once you have defined success for yourself, you have taken your first stumbling, awkward baby steps. No easy road lies ahead of you; there are no traffic-light-less thruways with signs pointing out: SUCCESS, 50 MILES. You must be your own navigator, and your compass is in your mind.

But your built-in "success instinct" is on your side. All animals have these instincts which help them to deal successfully with their environments, guaranteeing their survival. And man's success instinct is much more developed than that of animals. God blessed man with prime equipment for the achievement of success. For animals do not choose their goals —reproduction, self-preservation, food gathering—they are all instinctive.

Man, however, has the power of creative imagination, a

power that animals do not possess. More than a mere creature, he is a creator. Utilizing the imaging ability of his imagination, he can set his own goals. He can be master of his own ship; he can choose to go to Europe or the South Seas. He can select his own target, take dead aim on it, and direct his energies to hitting the bull's-eye.

In addition, man can then rely on his marvelous, built-in success mechanism to take over for him once the stage has been set for it. You have this wonderful mechanism geared to aid you; just whirl it into positive motion!

First, choose your goals—but make sure they are *your* goals. Too many people kid themselves and really aim at what they think other people want them to achieve. They are not the master of their ship. They are galley slaves shoveling coal into the ever-hungry furnace and, though they may shovel furiously, sweat pouring down their backs, the ship they are propelling forward is not theirs. *Even if they succeed, they will fail,* for they are slave labor.

But once you have probed into your own mind and your own heart and you know what it is that *you* want, then you are on your way to success that is genuine. You are a free man, a unique creature in the eyes of God, and when you wake up in the morning, you have goals. You are on your way to a successful day!

Remember, first, select goals that are *yours*. Second, be sure that they are realistic in terms of your talents and the world you live in. Third, visualize your goals and use your creative imagination to direct you toward their realization.

You Have as Many Rights as the Next Fellow

On our security exchanges, traders buy and sell the stock of business corporations. When a stock is selling at $100 a share and a trader thinks it is worth $50, he may sell short. He feels the stock is overvalued; he anticipates that other people will see this too. If he sells short, he hopes to make a profit if the market price of the stock declines.

But too many people sell themselves short, and they do not make a profit out of it at all. Quite the contrary! They lose their shirts; they treat their own aspirations with contempt, despising themselves, pouring cancer into their souls.

We come to a basic concept here. You, reading this chapter, have gone over it carefully so far. You've defined success for yourself, you've thought of goals you really want that are also reasonable for you; you've even figured out a few ways to go about things and pictured them in your imagination. *But, if you sell yourself short, you will fail!*

Millions of people in their hearts feel they were born to be failures. If success were handed them on a silver platter, they would find a way to fail. They do not feel that they have the right to succeed; success would be criminal. In their minds are rows and rows of freshly plowed fields waiting for harvest. But the crop is failure!

Have you ever tried raising your own food? It's fun, lots of people get a kick out of it! But, when you plant lettuce seeds, will you get asparagus? Of course not! But, by the same token, when you plant the seeds of failure, how can you hope to get success?

You must replant your mind, inserting seeds of success, seeds labeled the "will to win." You must realize that you have as many rights as the next fellow, no matter how successful he is.

People have ingenious ways of failing, ways that are hard to believe. I know one man who inherited apartment buildings worth perhaps a half million dollars. Feeling he was unworthy, however, he neglected them, forgot to collect the rent and, inside of a few years, threw away $70,000. Luckily, he realized his will to fail and righted himself before he destroyed all his good fortune.

A patient of mine felt comfortable as an economic failure, but made the mistake of making a lot of money. Immediately he developed anxieties. He became a hypochondriac, was afraid other people were out to rob him of his money. He visited doctors, took out insurance, worried all the time—it was no good. He preferred failure to success.

One woman came to my office seeking plastic surgery on her nose. There was nothing wrong with it; it would have been a crime for me to operate and I refused to do so. She was just trying to destroy herself unconsciously.

It seems to me that many people who fail regard success and money as the same thing. This is a serious mistake. A successful person may not have a dime in the bank. Real wealth is in a person's heart. It may be associated with the making of money—or it may not.

But one thing that all successful people share is a belief that they deserve to be happy, that happiness is their very birthright, that the sun rises each morning to usher in a day of successful living.

Successful People: How They Did It!

The great movie star Clark Gable was this kind of person. You've all seen moving pictures he starred in. He portrayed cocky, cheerful men who enjoyed life.

Before he became well known, Gable lived this way. He was never afraid to try new things; he enjoyed new adventures. He was a water boy in a mine and a timekeeping clerk in a steel products plant. After World War I, he worked part time in a clothing store. When about 20, he was a garage mechanic and later worked long hours learning to be a tool dresser. He tried acting for a stock company, spending two years with a tent show at $10 a week. Later he worked as a lumberjack.

These were not years of failure leading up to fabulous triumphs, for Gable was a success even then. To him success and living dynamically were synonymous, so even while he was economically poor Gable was successful.

To Harlow Curtice, former president of General Motors, success has centered largely around forceful drive in economic areas.

A country boy, Curtice had little more than a high school diploma when in 1914 he got a bookkeeper's job with a partly owned subsidiary of General Motors. At 35 he was president of the company. Curtice was only 40 when he was appointed general manager of General Motors' prized Buick division.

Curtice has always relished action. A dynamic executive, he pressed for daring designs on the new models, revised Buick sales channels and traveled across the country to see

Buick dealers, giving them faith in the product they were selling.

During four years in the middle of the depression, he quadrupled sales of Buick cars, installing his division as the second biggest money-maker in the General Motors setup.

Curtice's success netted him a salary of about $750,000 a year, but it was even greater than this enormous salary indicates. He enjoyed setting goals for himself and his subordinates, took delight in overcoming the obstacles that cropped up, and developed the habit of winning.

Charles Allen is a man who made it big in the world of finance. Quitting school at 15 to become a Wall Street runner, he began his own investment house at 19. Unbelievably, he made and lost close to a million dollars by the time he was 26.

Allen's success was based on a belief in his ability to evaluate securities; this confidence helped him to invest large sums of money. Able to make vital decisions quickly, he could speak out when millions of dollars were at stake.

Allen never let temporary failure throw him. Initially he had neither money nor connections, and he made a fortune only to go under in the stock market crash. Some men committed suicide during these grim days, but he wasn't floored. Building up his business once again, he made his banking house wealthy and influential.

Althea Gibson, the Negro tennis star, wrote a book called *I Always Wanted to Be Somebody* (Harper & Row, 1958), in which she described her concept of success: "I always wanted to be somebody. I guess that's why I kept running away from home when I was a kid even though I took some terrible whippings for it. It's why I took to tennis right away and kept working at it, even though I was the wildest tomboy you ever saw and my strong likings were a mile away from what the tennis people wanted me to do.

". . . I was determined that I was going to be somebody, too—if it killed me."

Althea's will to win was so strong that she became a "somebody," one of the big names in women's tennis for a number of years.

Romain Gary, the great French novelist, felt that his success would repay a mother he loved; she had given him tenderness and devotion. Through his art he felt he was giving to his mother *something that he wanted to give her*.

In *Promise at Dawn* (Harper & Row, 1961), Gary wrote:

"I knew that my mother's own artistic ambitions had never been fulfilled and that she was dreaming for me of a career she had never known herself. . . .

"I was determined to do all I could to make her, by proxy, so to speak, through my achievements, a famous and acclaimed artist: it was only a matter of choosing the right field; and, having hesitated for a long time among painting, acting, singing, and dancing, after many a heartbreaking failure, we were finally driven to literature, which has always been the last refuge, in this world, for those who do not know where to lay their dreaming heads."

To most people today, the name Houdini is synonymous with the word "magician" and the very act of magic. His story is enlightening because he was a self-made man who worked very hard at his craft, keeping faith in himself even in the midst of defeats.

Houdini was comparatively unknown for many years, working in the circus, beer halls and vaudeville. Tirelessly, he kept practicing his magical feats. His family opposed him, the world did not recognize him but he kept going, improving his trade, until he finally achieved renown as a magician.

To some men today baseball means success and centerfielder Jimmy Piersall has been a successful ballplayer for many years.

Piersall, once a high-strung young player on the Boston Red Sox, broke down under emotional strain. He did this while in the public eye—major league baseball players are potential headline-makers for newspapers—and could have quit baseball to avoid personal embarrassment. Jimmy was a fighter, however, and came right back to play more than 10 years in the American League, a target for those who attend baseball games to bait ballplayers, and he even hit .322 for the Cleveland Indians in 1961.

Success doesn't always come easy. Sometimes winning in life takes a lot of good, old-fashioned courage.

Believe in Yourself and You'll Succeed

Ralph Waldo Emerson once wrote that "Self trust is the first secret of success" and certainly this is true. But some people connect success with "luck." The winners, they say, are those who are "lucky."

I do not believe in "luck" and I think it is a dangerous concept, for once a person believes that he is "unlucky," he is very likely to give up on life. It's true that some days seem to go better than others, things may be more to one's liking, but these factors even themselves out over the long run. Too often, the person who believes in "luck" is waiting for someone to help him out, instead of having the confidence in himself to take the initiative.

I've already gone over some of the ingredients of success, but one maxim is basic: *Believe in yourself and you'll succeed!*

The successful people I've written about in this chapter are so different—in their concepts of success, their fields of endeavor, their strengths and weaknesses—but they all have one thing in common: a belief in themselves. In some of these people, this belief was at war with failure instincts and they had to fight to win out, but this belief in themselves was part of their personalities.

There is nothing in this world which you need to live successfully which is beyond your grasp.

According to Edmund Burke, the great eighteenth century British statesman, "Those things which are not practicable are not desirable. There is nothing in the world really beneficial that does not lie within the reach of an informed understanding and a well directed pursuit."

Yes, but with one *if*—if you believe in yourself, if you think that you are the kind of person who deserves success and happiness.

But not many of us live up to our potentials.

In an article entitled "Man's Potential and His Performance" in the *New York Times* Sunday magazine of November 24, 1957, Dr. Joseph W. Still writes:

"The charts reproduced here are based on observation of human physical and intellectual behavior made during 9 years of research in gerontology, the study of aging. They indicate the potential of normal men and women as compared with their usual performance. Each contains an upper 'success' curve and a lower 'failure' curve. I believe that not more than 5% of the population follow the upper curve. The rest fail for lack of motivation and understanding of their abilities.

"First as to the chart of physical growth. No one can doubt that the 'failure' curve represents the physical development of a great many people today. They get almost no physical exercise. They eat and drink and smoke too much. Their physical fitness declines rapidly after the early thirties.

"As for the chart of psychological growth. Again we have a 'failure' curve which describes the intellectual development of far too many today. Too many people reach the peak of curiosity and intellectual growth in high school or college or in early adult life and cease growing and begin to decline."

Why does this informed observer find a "failure" curve instead of a "success" curve? There is something wrong when so many people reach their intellectual peak so early. Life should be a process of continuing growth until death.

The answer is that too many of us don't believe in ourselves. We watch baseball games on television when we might be better off playing baseball. We watch soap operas on television instead of living full lives ourselves. We have come to be "watchers" instead of "doers" and have thus lost faith in our creative powers. We are becoming passive people who observe life while it passes us by.

To be one of life's winners, you must recapture your belief in yourself. You must set worthwhile goals for yourself and believe in their worth—no matter how insignificant these goals might seem to someone else.

No One Is Perfect

Remember that old proverb: *If at first you don't succeed, try, try again.* I think I first heard these words when I was a little boy in public school, and I never heard truer words. We can all learn from it, too.

If you feel that you must succeed all the time, you will be a failure—for no one is perfect.

The housewife who feels her house must be perfectly clean will be miserable all her life. Homes are not sterilized test tubes. No one can make them antiseptic.

The schoolboy who feels he must get "A" in every subject cannot win. Life is just not perfect. Even if his mastery of every subject is commanding, he will sooner or later have a teacher who rarely gives students "A" grades.

The man who feels he should never show emotion is just building a wall around himself. He is not being noble or perfect; he is imprisoning his success mechanism.

The woman who thinks all her features should be classically perfect is degrading her human qualities, turning herself into a puppet.

The night watchman who berates himself every day of his life because he isn't a doctor is being a traitor to his positive qualities.

Now, let's get back to our proverb. Many people can't succeed at things, because they won't even try. They are afraid of failure; they must be perfect even the first time they attempt something. If their perfectionism is really extreme, they will try nothing new—for at first they might not succeed.

Perfectionism is an enemy to success.

To Err Is Only Human

You cannot succeed at anything if you don't treat yourself as a human being. And a human being makes mistakes. To err is only human; if you were really perfect, you'd have no friends. No one could relax with you.

All babies, learning to walk, stumble and fall. Do we call them failures? Of course not. We readily see that walking is at times difficult for them and expect them to make trial-and-error progress.

But suppose you have to do something that's equally difficult for you, at your present level of maturity. Suppose

57

you're a housewife and your husband brings the boss home to dinner—and you've never been in this situation before. You're more nervous than usual and make a joke that just doesn't come off and, getting flustered, ask a question that is embarrassing or tactless. You've erred; are you a failure?

Of course you're not. You're a human being who faced a trying situation and stumbled. Why shouldn't you have as much compassion for yourself as you do for a baby trying something new?

Forget your failure and try to do your best to make the remainder of the evening pleasant. The boss might even like you—and your husband—better because he sees you're human. You don't know what his problems are.

As the great English poet John Dryden once wrote:

> Presence of mind and courage in distress
> Are more than armies to procure success.

Just as a housewife wants to fulfill her functions successfully, so does the young married man want to prove himself as the breadwinner. The baby is only two months old, it's their first child, and never before has he felt such desire to support his newly enlarged family. But along with the desire goes a feeling he's not familiar with—pressure.

He's been an insurance salesman for 18 months and he's done well for a beginner, but the pressure changes his personality a little. He's more anxious when he deals with a customer, more forcing in attitude, thinks of his own need for money rather than the customer's need for insurance. He blames himself for messing up a few sales he should have made and soon thinks of himself as a failure.

Is he? Certainly not. He's going through a period of readjustment and is temporarily disturbed. *His only real mistake is that he is not accepting his mistakes.*

Problems are a big part of life and, to live successfully, one must live with them. Pressure, mistakes, tensions, misjudgments—these are parts of life too, the lot of a *human* being. Sometimes all of us feel inadequate to the demands made upon us.

The Roman Publilius Syrius once wrote, "If you wish to

reach the highest, begin at the lowest," and this is not bad advice.

If You Don't Like Yourself, Who Will?

In this chapter, I've given you a few ideas which can help you to make yourself a winner. If you work hard on the practice exercise following, I'm sure that you will also find this helpful.

In the long run, it is your self-image which is the determining factor. Your success or failure rides with the adequacy of your self-image. In Chapter 1, I describe a type of salesman who simply will not sell well; his self-image is too weak.

He can change—and so can you. You can change your self-image and become more successful in life if you see the truth about yourself, if you use your imagination to see yourself as you've been at your best and project yourself through imagery into playing new roles that are within the limits of your physical and emotional capabilities. If you can relax and accept your weaknesses, if you can feel compassion for yourself as a human being alone in the universe—such a small part of the scheme of things—you can see what is good in yourself and stop torturing yourself with what is negative.

For it is this pictorial concept of oneself as a failure that makes one fail.

And it is this generous, loving, giving self-image which basically makes a person successful and happy.

This does not imply idealization of oneself. We are all struggling in a world full of problems and we simply do the best we can to live each day givingly. We all have faults and we try to overcome them; sometimes we can, sometimes we can't. Most of us have friends and enemies.

If anyone should be your friend, it should be you! If you don't like yourself, who will?

And, if you are your own friend, if your self-image makes sense, if you know what you want and set your sights on realistic goals, using your imagination to guide your efforts— you will be a winner!

Practice Exercise No. 3: How to Achieve Success

In this exercise, I will suggest concrete ways for you to attain your life goals.

1. *Encourage your success mechanism* by discarding your negative, "failure" thoughts; instead picture yourself as a success. Recapture, in your mind, every happy experience that you can bring to consciousness. Do not indulge in vague positive thinking; *picture* your moments of triumph. See them in technicolor; make them live again in your mind. Rise above images of failure; image, instead, how you will overcome your obstacles.

2. *Set definite, realistic goals for yourself.* After you've determined what you want, visualize the steps you must take to accomplish your objective. Don't let past failures discourage you! If your goals are within range of your potential, they make sense. Your success mechanism needs goals to function at its maximum efficiency.

3. *Understand your rights.* Many people think along these lines: "I've had this same dull job for 12 years but I don't deserve any better." Or "All I do in my spare time is watch TV, but I guess I just have no get-up-and-go." If you think in these channels, your trouble is that you do not have a high enough opinion of yourself; you do not feel that you have the same rights as successful people. As a matter of fact, often the difference between success and failure is one's conviction of what he deserves. Tell yourself that you are a deserving person. Think of people you regard as successes and tell yourself that you have the same rights they have. Keep on thinking about this concept until you feel the truth which, in different words, is part of our great American Declaration of Independence: that each of us has rights to the good things of life.

4. *Believe in yourself.* If you feel that you have too many faults, that you've made too many mistakes in life, remember that no one is perfect. The whole business of being successful is to rise above failure. To achieve success without problems confronting you is one thing. To achieve success by overcoming failure and rising above it is a far greater victory, for in

that very act you improve your self-image and your stature of self-respect. Tell yourself, again and again, that your failures are in the past; that, beginning right now, you will be a success.

5

You Can Master Your Habits and Control Your Destiny

There's an old saying that we are all "creatures of habit" and I think that this is quite true. We all tend to follow certain habit patterns in leading our lives.

Some habits are culturally determined. Almost everyone shares them in a given society. If you live in the U.S.A., for example, I can predict that, when you wake up in the morning, one of the first things you do is brush your teeth. Most Americans have this habit—and it's a good one. Your breath smells better, your teeth are healthier and your mouth feels fresher.

Some habits are more individual. A friend of mine, with whom I now and then debate a philosophical question, invariably gestures with his pipe when he makes a point. He has done this for as long as I can remember him.

If your habits are wholesome, you *must be* a happy person. If they are not, you should make every effort to change them—so that you can live a fuller, more vivacious life.

Some people say that "you can't teach an old dog new tricks." I don't believe this at all. You can change—it's just more difficult, because first one must undo negative habit patterns that have been part of the individual for many years.

In writing this chapter I aim to help you to cement your good habits and to replace your poor habits with ones that will make your life happier and more successful.

The word "habit" is a negative one to many people. In this age of materialism and loss of moral and spiritual vision, with playwrights and authors writing about heels and destructive people, with good people no longer considered interesting, we hear about the "drinking habit," "smoking habit," "drug habit."

But habits can be good, even inspiring, and the whole art of living is to overcome bad habits and rise above them to habits that make for a good life.

The Importance of Habit

Your habits govern your life, and you need them to function in the world. To give an elementary example, upon waking up on a weekday morning, you habitually brush your teeth, wash yourself, put on your clothes, button them, and eat some kind of breakfast. If you hadn't developed these and other socially acceptable habits, you would not be tolerated in your community.

Without the aid of habits, you would be slowed down to a walk in your daily activities. You would be in conflict with yourself about the simplest functions. You would need a full 24 hours to get your day's work done and you'd have no time for sleep.

Are you a housewife? Where would you be if you forgot how to cook breakfast for your husband, make the beds, and wash the dishes?

Are you a department store salesman? Where would you be without the habits of dressing neatly, greeting your customers politely, and knowing the prices of the merchandise?

But, useful as some habits are, others may be destructive. The person who automatically smokes three packs of cigarettes every day has formed a habit that is his implacable enemy.

How Habits Are Born

The child, growing up, learns ways of doing things from his parents and later from his friends. Soon these actions and thinking tools become part of him; they become automatic. He repeats them again and again for months and years, perhaps for the rest of his life.

Habit patterns operate not only in an action, such as tying one's shoelaces or driving a car. Our emotional reactions and feelings also depend on habit patterns.

You can develop the good habit of thinking of yourself as a worthwhile, constructive citizen with goals for every day of your life. Or you can think of yourself as a failure, a person of no worth—and this way of thinking is a habit.

In *The Road to Emotional Maturity* (Prentice-Hall, 1958) Dr. David Abrahamsen writes:

"All of our habits, in fact, express something basic in us, since they reflect our unconscious feelings. This is the reason why we do not think of the way we eat, talk, or walk, or the way we carry out our daily routine.

"Pavlov's simple experiments with dogs were the first proof that habits were the result of pre-conditioned responses to given stimuli, and that these habits would continue even when the situation no longer remained exactly the same.

"To prove this theory, he held out a piece of meat to a dog and rang a bell at the very same moment. At the sight of the meat, the dog's salivary glands began to work. Each time Pavlov repeated this procedure, the dog reacted in the same way. Eventually, no meat was offered—only the bell was rung. The dog's glands still secreted the saliva, because his reaction had become automatic and spontaneous—it was unconscious. It would be a long time before this repetitive pattern of action could be dissociated from the original factors that related to it.

"And so we see that while we accept our habits as a definite part of us which was always there, when in reality they were acquired as we grew up. . . ."

Just as Pavlov's dogs were conditioned, so are people. You can think of yourself as a winner or a loser; either way of thinking is a habit pattern that can jet-propel you toward life or force you to retreat into a shell.

I know of a girl with great talent as a pianist who has gotten into the habit of thinking that she was incompetent. A friend told me the story of how this girl, when younger, used to perform brilliantly at the piano keyboard, her ability outstanding. Yet if she made one small mistake, her mother would scold her.

Today she criticizes herself for the slightest mistake, putting her wonderful talent in a strait jacket. Her negative habit of extreme perfectionism has ruined a career that had every possible potential.

And so, in our childhood, habits are formed and they persist a long time. *But you can change them and, in this chapter, I'll show you how.*

Stop Drinking—and Start Living!

Drinking is a self-destructive habit. I don't mean the custom of taking a drink or two after work to ease the pressures of the day—I see nothing wrong with drinking in moderation. I mean the habit of turning to the bottle in any crises and swallowing drink after drink in a frantic effort to escape from life. This is known as "alcoholism."

People often mistakenly think of alcoholics as happy, imagining the "happy drunk" they may have seen in a movie. Actually, though, when the consumption of alcohol is a habit which the individual can no longer fight, it is a terrible disease. The movie "Days of Wine and Roses," which shows the sufferings of an alcoholic married couple, is a classic picturing of the tragic consequences of alcoholism.

The attraction of alcohol is that, under its influence, one can escape from the outer and inner world of problems into a dream world—for a while. A few drinks, and you can forget all about income taxes and parking tickets and that argument with your mother-in-law. A few more drinks, and you'll even forget about how inferior you feel on the job. A few more, and if the atomic bomb went off in your face, you'd grin stupidly.

If you're troubled, however, your relief is only temporary. The next day your head will feel as if carpenters had assaulted it with hammers. Your "escape" from reality did not bring you joy. Over the long run, drinking heavily will dull your senses, and ruin your physical constitution.

People who drink habitually do so to escape from more

than realistic pressures; they are running away from a negative concept of themselves, a feeling of inferiority that obsesses them.

The drinking habit is a pernicious one and, if you drink too much, you should see this clearly and work to change your ways. Before you can break a habit, however, you must admit that it exists.

Alcoholics Anonymous, which has helped people break the drinking habit, asks that its members begin talks to groups announcing, "I am an alcoholic." This admission is important, for many alcoholics insist on kidding themselves, telling themselves that they are not alcoholics, but just "social drinkers."

Dr. Harry J. Johnson, in *The Life Extension Foundation Guide to Better Health* (Prentice-Hall, copyright Life Extension Foundation, 1959.) writes that: "An authoritative study, which dug into the history of more than 5,000 families and covered three to five generations, once yielded the conclusion that moderate drinking did not shorten life span by a single day. Neither, however, did it increase life span. I merely want to point out these facts, because there are so many fallacies in circulation regarding drinking. All existing evidence strongly endorses the potential benefit to be derived from an occasional drink."

So don't be afraid to take an occasional drink! There's a vast gulf between the bona fide social drinker and the true alcoholic.

But, if drinking is really a habit with you, you must resolve to break the pattern. Later on in this chapter, I will give you tools to help you stop drinking and start living!

Think Yourself Thin!

Another common American scourge is overeating. The twin to this habit is the condition of overweight, which sends many people on sporadic diets from which they emerge, hungrier than ever, to knife-and-spoon their way back to their pre-diet weight.

Comedians find good material for humor in kidding people who are overweight, but it is not really funny.

According to Dr. Johnson, "Long life and excess weight do

66

not go together. Overweight is perhaps the greatest health hazard of the twentieth century. It is like a plague. There is overwhelming evidence that for each ten percent increase in overweight, mortality increases by 20 percent.

"Overweight, as a cause of death, does not show up on mortality tables. But I believe—and so do most of my medical colleagues—that it is directly and indirectly responsible for more disability and illness than any single disease. Heart disease, kidney disease, strokes, and diabetes occur two and a half times as frequently among people 25 percent over normal weight than among those of the same age with normal weight.

"In more than nine out of ten cases, excess weight is caused by nothing more than eating too much. Only rarely is it the result of some organic disease."

This is not a pretty picture and one might well ask, "Why do people eat too much? Why don't they know when to stop?"

The answer is simply that it has become a habit with them, one which provides temporary satisfaction and which they thus hate to renounce. People whose lives are full do not eat too much. They *feed* themselves with goals that are worthwhile and activities that are exciting. They *nourish* themselves with giving relationships to other people and with the feeling that each day is an adventure. They relax with themselves and sleep the sleep of happy people, and need only a normal amount of food to eat.

If you eat too much, and are overweight, your overeating habit is a result of an emotional grievance, conscious or buried. You overeat to make up for what you feel you are missing or have missed at some time in your life. You are trying to soothe all your frustrations with food, and it can't be done.

Keep reading, and I'll give you some hints on how to "think yourself thin."

Don't Smoke too Much!

Smoking is a habit that has a hold on many people, who puff away day after day on cigarettes, pipes, and cigars. Cigarette smoking is, to my knowledge, the most common and there have been studies attempting to connect cigarette smoking with cancer, heart conditions and other serious diseases. Amazingly, these studies have not broken the national habit. I don't think they've even made a dent in it.

The American Cancer Society and the Public Health Service have both published statistics which seem to demonstrate a relationship between cigarette smoking and disease. *Reader's Digest* surveys have also suggested a link between cigarette smoking and lung cancer.

An American Cancer Society study on the smoking habits of 188,000 men between the ages of 50 and 70 years disclosed a frightening coronary death rate for smokers—some 70 percent higher than the rate for non-smokers.

The Reader's Digest is a widely read magazine, with a circulation of over 23,000,000 at this writing, but its findings seem to have gone unheeded. Many people *need* to smoke; smoking cigarettes relieves their tensions.

Cigarette smoking, I believe, also artificially helps many people to think well of themselves. The endless repetition of TV cigarette commercials has had its desired effect: a young lady puffing daintily on a cigarette may identify herself with the smiling blonde standing by a waterfall, her hair blowing in the breeze; a young man exhaling vigorously may think himself the brother of the muscular six-footer who showed all his teeth in the 60-second break.

Aside from the danger of relying on a habit that may be injurious to your health, this is no way to strengthen your self-image, because it is artificial and in most cases unrealistic. Your self-image must be made of stone and mortar, not of smoke floating away into the air.

I do not think smoking an occasional cigarette can hurt anyone physically; but when it becomes a habit and a person must run through two packs a day to exist, then it can be dangerous, if we are to believe medical reports.

How do you stop smoking?

In *How to Stop Killing Yourself,* Dr. Peter J. Steincrohn (Wilfred Funk, revised and enlarged edition, 1962.) writes: "Here is a helpful trick for the inveterate cigarette smoker. Recognize that for most of us, smoking is a reflex action. The easiest way to break a habit is to substitute another one for it. Keep pieces of hard candy on hand. Whenever you have the urge to smoke, reach for the sweet instead of the cigarette. The reaching, the unwrapping of the candy, the putting it into your mouth, the sucking on it—not to mention the slight rise of blood sugar that ensues—are series of reflexes equivalent to reaching for the pack, removing a cigarette, lighting it, and puffing. Try it. It is a pleasant way to fool your reflexes. And it works."

Don't Work Yourself to Death!

A full person has good work habits. As a member of the community, one can often make his greatest contribution to others through his work. A person who doesn't work will usually feel like a parasite; he will probably think little of himself and others will most likely confirm his opinion.

But some people habitually *overwork* themselves. They work long hours in their offices and, when the working day is done, they carry home briefcases filled with papers so they can continue their work at home. Work is not part of their life; *their life is work.*

This is too great a burden for a mere human being. To live well, a person should work, relax, sleep. He should devote time and attention to each part of this threefold daily schedule. All work and no play does a man no good in the long run, and he may be heading for an early heart attack.

Why do people overwork? *First,* because they are slaves to the idea of great material success. *Second,* because through continual work, they can escape the problems they have with themselves and other people.

John Tebbel, in *The Magic of Balanced Living* (Harper & Row, 1956), writes:

"Running like a strong current beneath all the discussions of work and health is the 'success' fallacy that dominates American life. Most men have to contend with it, and they had better recognize the enemy as early as possible if they are not to be defeated by it.

"It is both a fallacy and an enemy. No one is a success who has made a great deal of money and hasn't the time or the good health to enjoy it. The record is full of 'successes' who single-mindedly pursued the goal of success, achieved it in their late forties or early fifties, and died of a heart attack or succumbed to another disease generated by worry, anxiety and tension. Of course it is quite possible to be both successful and healthy, but the percentage of American men who have achieved that goal is small."

Remember this: *If success to you means material success and vocational attainment, more power to you! See yourself as a success and go out and achieve your goals. But to overwork and overdrive yourself, to ruin your health and exceed your limitations—this is folly!*

Some people accept themselves only when they're working. Outside of work, they are at a loss; they do not know how to relate to the world of people except through work. In overworking themselves, they satisfy a need to prove that they are worthwhile human beings. In doing so, they can ruin their health. The tragedy is that they are worthwhile, as people, and don't even know it.

If you overwork yourself, tell yourself that you live only once and that there is more to life than work. Live each day as if it were your last! Resolve to face the problems that drive you away from your true self and into work. Redefine your concepts of success, developing your full emotional qualities as well as your work abilities.

Dress as if You Think You're Worth It

The way you dress is another of your most important habits. While clothes do not necessarily make the man, people will often judge you—sometimes unfairly—by your personal appearance. When you dress well, you present a positive picture of yourself to the world. Nowadays many people pay too much attention to clothes, ignoring spiritual qualities that make us bigger people. Still, if you are a sloppy dresser, you have acquired a negative habit. You are putting your worst foot forward.

It does not take great effort to dress neatly and, if you are habitually slovenly, you should ask yourself why you think you are so worthless—for you must think this. When you think more of yourself, as you should, you will take the trouble to dress as if you thought you were worth it.

You Can Change Your Habits

Now I'm going to get down to brass tacks and tell you how you can change your bad habits. But, first, *you must believe that this is possible.*

In an October, 1957, article, *Science Digest* relates an experiment in which about one half of a group of 57 college student nailbiters cured themselves of this habit or showed marked improvement, in less than a year.

The late Dr. Knight Dunlap devoted many years to studying habits and helped people stop nail-biting and thumb-sucking.

Alcoholics Anonymous has helped great numbers of suffering souls break away from a habit that was ruining their lives. The U.S. Health Service at Lexington, Ky., has even helped sufferers from the dread drug addiction to regain their pride and self-control and lick the habit.

Surely each of you knows one person who has dragged himself out of a rut of negativism and developed new, successful ways of thinking.

You can change your habits. It's not as easy as rolling off a log, but you can do it. If you really want to. Your negative habits stand between you and happiness. Why not write them off? Why go around in the same circle when it leads you nowhere?

If you eat too much or drink too much, or if other bad habits plague you, and you want to change them, here's what you do:

1. *Believe that you can change your habit.* Have faith in your ability to control yourself and to bring about positive changes in your basic makeup.

2. *Understand the physical consequences* of these habits so well that you're willing to undergo temporary deprivations— even suffering—so great is your desire to change. Face the reality that being overweight puts a strain on your vital organs, that alcohol undermines your tissues, that overwork might drive you into premature death, and so forth.

3. *Find something satisfying* which will comfort you during the temporary period of pain that you will go through while you are depriving yourself of a prop that has sustained you

for a long time. A hobby such as photography or gardening or piano playing might help wean you away from, say, smoking too much.

4. *Discover the basic problems* that drove you to such excesses. What is your frustration? Do you undervalue yourself? Why are you such an enemy to yourself?

5. *Come to grips with these problems.* Realign your thinking; accept your failures and rediscover your triumphs.

6. *Direct yourself toward positive habit patterns* that will make your life rewarding. Set new goals for yourself. Get the feel of success in constructive activities that will bring out your ability and your enthusiasm.

If you will have faith in the potency of these concepts, and dedicate yourself to applying them, you can change any type of negative habit pattern. You can thrust aside the bottle that brings more pain than satisfaction, or the extra helping of strawberry shortcake which will never really console you for your past deprivations. Go over my suggestions once more and, when your will falters, read them again and again. They will work for you if you have faith and patience, and if you're willing to work to achieve the results you want.

You can change your habits and lead a better life if you'll stop relying on miracles and get in the habit of realizing that you've got to work to get what you want.

The Most Important Habits of All

You can develop good habits that will improve your self-image.

A child finds that his parents brush their teeth in the morning and imitates them until it becomes second nature. He also learns to tie his shoes before going to school. Soon he can perform these functions automatically and he can think about a problem in his chemistry or physics course while he is brushing his teeth.

When he grows up, he can eat his breakfast, tie his shoes and think of his job responsibilities at the same time without straining—because his habits are sound.

If these simple physical habits help a person, how much more valuable it is to develop more important ones: parents might teach a child to stop fighting with his brother or to respect his sister.

In any family, the inception of good habits takes place when parents teach the child that he is not alone in life and must respect not only his own wishes, but those of others.

The growing child should have as his proudest possession a habitual way of thinking: feeling self-respect and dignity. Schools develop habits in children—in arithmetic, geography, English, history—and these are fine but, more important, there should be a course at an early age teaching them respect—of themselves and others.

They should learn positive habits of thinking: how to feel successful, how to respect other people, how to feel compassion for one's fellow men.

Boy Scouts taking older people across the street have learned outgoing, friendly habits. If their heart is in what they're doing, they are rewarded—not by money, which is not everything—but with their own self-respect, and the fellow feeling of other people.

People are not born with courage. When one feels respect and compassion for others, then he'll fight for them against injustice—and this is the basis of courage. When a white man stands up for a mistreated Negro in the South, the threat of physical violence doesn't bother him.

Compassion, charity, self-respect—when you can reach these feelings, you will like yourself.

The habit of profiting by mistakes, getting a sense of self-direction, you're on the right track here. Driving toward your goals, driving toward them in spite of obstacles, is the beginning of habit—for habit is repetition.

One of the greatest habits to develop is that of accepting yourself for what you are, instead of pushing yourself to be what you're not, which is one of the worst habits in the world today. Accepting yourself as you are gives you confidence, whereas scrambling to keep up with the neighbors produces a sense of continual tension. It is a terrible undermining habit, and it will inflict cracks in the core of your self-image.

If you understand this, you realize that worry is a bad habit, just as happiness is a good quality. Happiness is the habitual glow of excitement you feel from your positive anticipations.

Resentment is a vicious habit because it is repetitious. Anger breeds fear of retaliation which brings on more anger and feelings of uncertainty—the vicious circle never ends. It does not pay. Resentment will hurt the person who is your victim, but it will inflict far greater harm on the person who hates.

If you have developed negative habits such as worrying, resenting, fearing, and dreading the future, it is important that you see clearly how these habits corrode your self-image. When you can visualize yourself as you really are, then you can work on changing the habits that destroy the dignity of your self-image.

What kind of person do you want to be? In the theater of your mind, project the witches of Macbeth, cackling as they stir the cauldron on the flames. You're the audience so you can visualize them clearly. Do you want to have their traits of maliciousness and sly cunning? Or would you rather have the nobility of a King Arthur of the Round Table?

It's all up to you, the person you will be. You can be witch or knight in shining armor. You can be Dr. Jekyll and Mr. Hyde, with good and bad coexisting, but you certainly would be more fortunate if you developed the kind of emotional habits that lead to happiness.

In the final analysis, habit represents the use of imagination, positive or negative. If you use your imagination as an ally, you will insure your well-being. It is *your* imagination and, if you feel that you have the rights of a valuable human being, you can use it to give you the emotional patterns that will make your life a joy.

Practice Exercise No. 4: Make Habit Your Friend

Your habits can be your friends or your enemies; they can help you or hurt you. Apply your energies to develop constructive habits, which will channel you into happy activities.

Here are three winning habits:

1. *Do the practice exercises in this book.* This is a wonderful habit to form. These exercises have a definite purpose: to help you think better of yourself and relax with a self-image that you like. I'm confident they will help you, but only if you get into the habit of doing them regularly—just like washing your hands or combing your hair. Understand that they are just as important; surely your self-image has as much meaning as your personal appearance and cleanliness.

2. *Understand the importance of your mind.* It is such an awesome force. The ideas I stress in this book—mental picturing, concepts of yourself and the world, attitudes toward success, happiness and people—are all products of your mind. They consist of thoughts and images, vague in that you can't see them.

You might, therefore, say to yourself, "It's just an image in my mind. How important can it be? I can't touch it and only I can see it. Maybe it really doesn't matter."

Don't fall into this trap! The pictures your mind produces are basic to your stature as a human being. Often the ability to produce and sustain a single mental picture can be more significant than the attainment of monetary success and its materialistic accompaniments.

Your concepts, your mental images—more than anything, they are *you*. Tell yourself over and over just how important are the workings of your mind.

3. *Realize the power of your self-image.* This is another intangible, but its power is also real. You rise or fall, succeed or fail, depending on your self-image. For your own good, don't forget this!

Get out of the habit of rationalizing away your defeats and then crawling into a shell of resentment at the world's failure to recognize you. First, *you* have to recognize the good in yourself.

Tell yourself again and again about the power of your self-image and get into the habit of working to improve your concept and image of yourself, for this is your great hidden wealth.

Let's take an outstanding case, that of our late President John F. Kennedy. Politics is no one-way street and during his career Kennedy met challenges and refused to buckle under them. What was his great secret? Obviously, the strength of his image of himself. If you ever saw President Kennedy making a speech, surely you could feel the relaxation in the man, the at-homeness even in front of TV cameras. Only a man who sees himself favorably can be so comfortable when the eyes of millions are on him and their ears hear his every word, sometimes with the fate of the world at stake.

As further testimony to the fantastic power of the mind's imagery, consider this: Months and months after his death, as you read this book, you can picture this man in your mind. Though he is dead, you can see him still, alive and vivid. In a sense, this power of your imagery keeps him alive. Thus, with newsreel tapes to refresh our memories, he will never die in the theater of our minds.

Why not apply this same power of mental picturing to your advantage? Use this overwhelming impact to see yourself in your most successful moments, upgrading instead of downgrading yourself. Do not let your successes die; keep them alive in the theater of your mind! Keep on picturing your victories in life, doggedly focusing on your success pictures until they become a part of your personality and *what might have been* becomes *what is.*

6

Seven Rules for Happy Living

"It is one main point of happiness that he that is happy doth know and judge himself to be so," wrote Samuel Taylor Coleridge, the great English poet.

If you're happy, you'll know it. You'll feel it in your bones; you'll find excitement where some people find boredom.

Everyone has this right: to know what it feels like to be happy. You don't need to earn this right. You were born with it.

Our great Declaration of Independence affirmed this right. Written mostly by Thomas Jefferson, it asserted that "We hold these truths to be self-evident, that all men are created equal, that they are endowed by their creator with certain unalienable Rights, that among these are Life, Liberty and the pursuit of Happiness . . ."

But how many truly happy people do you know? Answer this question honestly. Use the fingers of your hands to count them; unless you know very unusual people, your ten fingers will be adequate for the task.

You Live Only Once

Whenever I think of the many unhappy people in the world, I find it amazing. Surely God did not mean us to spend our days in misery; life is too short for that. As human beings, we are God's proudest creatures. *We should be happy.*

You live only once—remember this when you're feeling blue. Make the most of your days; dedicate your energies to making yourself and others happy. Instead of sitting around moping, thinking of ways to waste time, understand the great value of time. Would you throw away money, if you were in your right mind? Of course not. Then why throw away time, which is also precious?

Time is one of your most treasured gifts. Alfred Lord Tennyson once wrote that

> . . . Time driveth onward fast,
> And in a little while our lips are dumb.

These are words to the wise. Don't waste your time, letting life pass you by.

Live Each Day as if It's Your Last

I know many people who live for the future. They are always saving for "a rainy day" or they are always putting their money away "so I can retire and go to Florida" or they work themselves to death "so I'll be taken care of when I'm older."

Foresight is a fine quality; I would not dream of criticizing it. Plans are fun and they're often wise. But—

Many of these people plan for the future *at the expense of the present*. This does not make sense to me. Life is uncertain, there are no guarantees, and a person who sacrifices the present for a future that might not ever come may be sacrificing his happiness.

If you can live each day richly and *still* lay the groundwork for a happy future, wonderful! But if you must surrender present joys, I say to you, "Don't do it!"

I speak from more than 60 years of experience in this world, some of it sad. And the saddest stories I know are of people who lived for "tomorrow" and died before they could ever reach it—or who saved for the "sunshine years" only to see unexpected expenses wipe out life savings—or who overworked themselves all their lives and arrived at the "golden years" with plenty of money but with their health shattered.

To live happily in the present and in the future:

1. *Live each day* as fully as you can.

2. *Set goals for every day.* Don't be afraid if some people think them trivial; if they have real meaning for you, that's all that counts.

3. *Tell yourself that you have the right to be happy;* don't let people worry you with their negative thinking.

4. *Set aside a number of hours for relaxation every day;* do the things that give you peace of mind and release from the practical problems of living.

5. *Accept yourself as you are,* with your strengths and weaknesses. Don't try to be someone else!

You could also try to *live each day as if it's your last.* If you image this to be true, you will shed minor irritations that ordinarily plague you. You will be surprised what a calming effect this thought can bring. You will stop worrying about the many little things that, added up, destroy happiness. For, on your last day on earth, why worry about trivia?

Happiness Is a State of Mind

Money's a nice thing to have but, in the final analysis, you can't buy happiness. You can however, think yourself into a state of happiness.

If you feel good about yourself and think you deserve to be happy, you will resolve to create happiness wherever you go.

If you want to be happy, you will find happiness all over the world. You will enjoy each bite of breakfast, your morning shower will be refreshing, you will feel content in the simple routine of getting dressed. When you go out into the street to go to work, you will feel happy to see your fellow human beings, because they are brothers. They are not perfect—are you?—and if some are unresponsive, you will understand that they may have problems that bother them. You will give to them the best you can and, if there is no immediate response, you will not care. Your act of giving will make you happy.

If it's raining, you will go to buy an umbrella and get enjoyment from the simple act of flicking it open and shut, appreciating its mechanical functioning with the simplicity of a child having fun with a toy.

There is much that is good in our imperfect world—if you want to see it with eyes that seek contentment.

Did you ever read Robert Louis Stevenson's short poem, "Happy Thought"?

> The world is so full of a number of things,
> I'm sure we should all be as happy as kings.

You can be "as happy as kings," but first you must think yourself into it. You must get rid of the negative feelings that are enemies of contentment: fear, worry, resentment. If you are infested with these phantom diseases, you cannot feel well and cannot know even what it means to be happy.

If a horde of mosquitoes were to invade your home, would you attempt to live with them? I doubt it. More likely you would spray them with insecticide or declare war with fly swatters—you might enlist the support of an exterminator. But negative thoughts are infinitely more dangerous. You cannot coexist with them, for they will not let you "live and let live." You must root them out and knock the props from under them; you must destroy them before they destroy you. Nazi Germany was a threat to world peace and her defeat in World War II was essential; so it is with negative thoughts, which are annihilators of your peace of mind.

You Can Be Happy if You Really Want to Be

Basically, it is your attitude toward yourself which determines whether you are happy or miserable. Do you see yourself as a weakling and a failure? You will be unhappy. Do you see yourself as a nice guy? You'll do fine.

You can be happy—if this is what you want for yourself.

A positive mental attitude—reinforced by your powerful mental imagery—will bring you all the success and happiness you desire. Such a positive attitude implies a feeling of faith, an impulse toward charity, and a dose of good common sense, and is topped off by the full potency of your imaginative processes.

These are qualities that will lead you toward happiness, provided your self-image is healthy enough to allow you joy in your days. Your concepts—about yourself and the world you live in—are powerful; it is sometimes difficult to comprehend just how powerful they are.

In *The Power of Your Subconscious Mind* (Prentice-Hall, 1963), Dr. Joseph Murphy tells of a man who wanted to be happy.

"A number of years ago, I stayed for about a week in a farmer's house in Connemarra on the west coast of Ireland. He seemed to be always singing and whistling and was full of humor. I asked him the secret of his happiness, and his reply was: 'It is a habit of mine to be happy. Every morning when I awaken and every night before I go to sleep, I bless my family, the crops, the cattle, and I thank God for the wonderful harvest.'"

Dr. Murphy also found that other people really craved misery.

"I knew a woman in England who had rheumatism for many years. She would pat herself on the knee and say, 'My rheumatism is bad today. I cannot go out. My rheumatism keeps me miserable.'

"This dear elderly lady got a lot of attention from her son, daughter, and the neighbors. She really wanted her rheumatism. She enjoyed her 'misery' as she called it. This woman did not really want to be happy."

He points out that "There is one very important point about being happy. You must sincerely *desire* to be happy. There are people who have been depressed, dejected, and unhappy for so long that were they suddenly made happy by some wonderful, good, joyous news, they would actually be like the woman who said to me, 'It is wrong to be so happy!' They have been so accustomed to the old mental patterns that they do not feel at home being happy! They long for the former, depressed, unhappy state."

The Habit of Contentment

In the last chapter, I talked to you about the importance of habit in your life. Happiness is a habit, a wonderful one. This is the kind of habit that you should try to develop.

I never met the farmer Dr. Murphy writes about, but probably he's not financially wealthy—few farmers are—and he's probably had his share of heartaches. The odds are that he's not much different from most of us, *but* he's developed the habit of reaching out for happiness. He sings and whistles while others worry about their troubles and complain to anyone willing to listen.

We all have troubles. Problems are part of life. They are always with us "and if it's not one thing, it's another."

But ask yourself this. When trouble comes, do you crawl into a shell of misery and resentment, or do you keep on whistling while you seek a solution? Do you mope and sit around feeling sorry for yourself or do you think back to better moments and plan for a successful future?

Your mind is such a potent tool. Remolding your truths, harnessing your imagination, driving yourself into the channels of success, you can use your mind to make you relaxed and happy. You can make contentment the essence of your life!

Laugh Your Troubles Away!

Get into the habit of laughing; too many of us have forgotten how to laugh. As people grow older, they sometimes forget that they ever laughed. It is a part of their childhood that they can no longer remember.

Did you ever see a happy baby? He crawls on the floor, picks up a toy and sticks it in his mouth, then drops it and gurgles delightedly. When he laughs, he opens his mouth wide in an expression of sheer, uninhibited joy. There is nothing halfhearted about the baby. He looks up at Mother and his whole face is a map of laughter. If she responds to his good nature, he lets out a howl of glee and claps his hands together and crawls ecstatically across the floor until another joyful object strikes his eye.

As grownups, our needs are much more complicated than a baby's. When a baby needs food, Mother comes with a bottle. When a grownup needs something, he often must be more patient until he reaches satisfaction and then must accept a compromise or even a defeat instead of what he really wanted. A grownup's life is usually demanding and at times frustrating.

Still, to laugh is to let joy bubble out to the world. We all feel joy sometimes and when we do, we should make the most of it, sharing it with other people, giving it a spirit and completeness that will make it last longer. Learn to laugh again —like a happy baby!

Sometimes, when you're feeling depressed over something that has defeated you, think of a past success or something funny that happened to someone else. Throw your head back—don't be afraid—and laugh, with all your heart and soul, and see if you don't feel better for it.

Accentuate Your Assets!

You can't laugh easily, however, if you dislike yourself. If you think poorly of yourself, you feel like crying, not laughing. So, first, you must build yourself up. Not artificially. That wouldn't do you any good at all. You can't kid yourself, and I am not advising you to be unrealistic. But you can build yourself up if you'll take a good, hard look at your own positive qualities.

You have them. I don't care who you are, they are there. They may be hidden, it is true, but you must dig them out and show them to yourself and to the world, so that you can feel pride in yourself and laugh once again.

I have, during my many years as plastic surgeon and human being, met so many people who buried their finest qualities: warmhearted, human men who felt forced to wear a mask of stoicism that cut them off from the world, to prove that they were masculine; women so ashamed of a mild facial deformity that they never dared to show their basic generosity; people so obsessed with vocational frustration that they downgraded all their other creative activities.

If your positive qualities are buried treasure, get out a pick and shovel and dig them out. Show them to yourself, so you can appreciate yourself, and then you'll be ready to take that treasure with you on the road to happiness.

Help Others, and Happiness Will Be Yours

Napoleon Hill and W. Clement Stone, in *Success Through a Positive Mental Attitude* (Prentice-Hall, 1960), write that "One of the surest ways to find happiness for yourself is to devote your energies toward making someone else happy. Happiness is an elusive, transitory thing. And if you set out to search for it, you will find it evasive. But if you try to bring happiness to someone else, then it comes to you."

This is basic truth. We are brothers and sisters, but too often we don't realize it and withdraw from each other, in our minds, or devote our energies to armed combat, in which we seek to outmaneuver each other—usually to gain material possessions which never give us the sense of joy we could experience in human kindness.

When you help others, you help yourself. You feel a sense of relatedness to others and others are your world. You feel that you are useful, that you are a meaningful person, a contributing member of society. In addition, if the people you help are appreciative (and most people are grateful for kindness), you feel the warmth of their reaction to you and your social interaction can be a friendly one. You feel more comfortable in the world of people and less need to retreat into an inner shell that is a living death.

To be happy, you must learn the art of give-and-take, which is the lifeblood of civilized living. The person who is just a "taker" can never be happy. A man whose whole life is grabbing money like a shark killer or a woman who accepts others' gifts like a pampered pet—neither can be happy in this kind of role. One must know the joy of giving, the spine-tingling thrill of making somebody else happy, to know the real meaning of contentment.

Happiness Is Contagious

I can't remember his exact words but an older friend, when I was growing up, once told me something like this, "When you are with negative-minded people, don't let their ideas take hold of you!"

This was good advice and I've tried to follow it, for negative thoughts are deadly; they are as contagious and as devastating as any bubonic plague that ever infested a population.

A few months ago, I was walking down the street, not far from my office in midtown New York. A casual acquaintance stopped me with a greeting.

"Hello," I said. "How are you?"

"Not so good. I was 60 last month and, you know, you get to feeling your age. You get to wondering how long you've got to live."

"I feel fine," I said, "I enjoy myself and I don't worry about that. And I'm past 60."

"Did you hear about —— ——?" he said. "Too bad. Cancer. He was only 54."

I expressed my regrets and asked him to convey them to the man's widow.

"Oh, well," he sighed. "The weather's so hot, it's unbearable anyway. Besides, the air's no good anymore with all these buses spewing out carbon monoxide. And, with income taxes coming up, life's too miserable to care about."

I shook hands with him, said goodbye and went back to my office. My nurse said a patient was waiting, so I erased the negative conversation from my mind and prepared to do something useful. But, if you let such negative people's thoughts take hold of your mind, you're a goner. You will waste your God-given days on this earth in worry.

Here's the main point, though: Just as misery loves company, so does happiness. When you are happy, you can spread it everywhere you go. You are a carrier of beauty and love, and you can give your gift to others.

Laughter is contagious when it's genuine. It can spread like wildfire through gloomy talk of nuclear annihilation, wiping the worry from people's minds and keeping your thoughts well-lubricated, ready for positive action.

Quiet happiness is also catching. When a person quietly gives another from his great storehouse of contentment, he makes the other person glad he's alive. His compassion turns suffering to acceptance and inhibition to expression of feelings. He turns worry to joy, and hate to love. The streets don't look dirty and paper-littered anymore; they look like efficient tools of transportation in a functioning civilization. The country fields don't look lifeless; they look mellow green with the throbbing growth of grass, watered by God's great natural force: rain.

Perform an Operation on Your Thoughts

When I was in my early twenties, studying to be a plastic surgeon, I learned to perform an operation that would improve a person's appearance. I learned how to handle nasal instruments, delicate tools that were used within the nostril in so small an area to remove a hump on a nose or to straighten a crooked nose—all done within the nostril to avoid an external scar.

I learned, in removing a scar and bringing the edges together, to be completely accurate with fine forceps that hold the skin edges while you bring them together with a very fine, curved needle and with stitches as fine as horsehair. I learned to bring these skin edges together with complete precision to prevent future scarring.

But you, too, can perform an operation—on your thoughts!

Don't laugh, because this is a tremendously important operation. The patient, you, can emotionally live or die. You need no surgical instruments, just the will to make yourself happy.

You will remove no scar tissue, just negative thoughts. You will try to cut out of your mind worry, fear, resentment, and replace them with thoughts that give you pleasure.

At the end of this chapter, you will find guides for making this happiness operation a success.

Activities That Bring Happiness

Your mind can function for your happiness; activities can also bring you fun.

Former President Dwight Eisenhower, when under the pressure of being Chief Executive, used golfing as a means of relaxation.

The late President John F. Kennedy, and others of this famous clan, played touch football and were strong advocates of physical fitness.

Britain's great Sir Winston Churchill has often painted natural scenes to bring him a few hours of quiet enjoyment in the midst of days of struggle.

The famous artist Grandma Moses, who lived to be one-hundred-and-one, took up painting as a relaxing hobby when she was in her eighties.

Hugh Downs, the TV personality, devotes much of his spare time to working for an association for the betterment of national health.

Bob Hope found rewards in traveling around the world entertaining our troops overseas during World War II.

Doing things will be fun for you—if you select the activities that *you* enjoy, and are not doing them to win the approval of other people. No one can tell you what to do; you know what you enjoy.

How a Politician Got Down to Brass Tacks

A friend of mine told me this story, and I think it's an instructive one. It's about a professional politician and his rise from misery to happiness.

This man had literally devoted his life to politics as a paid representative of a major political party. He talked politics every day in the week and he worked himself around the clock. He was a stranger to his wife and children; he provided for their material needs, but gave them no attention. He smoked and drank too much, to help his tension, but was able to keep going.

One year a cycle of trouble hit him. His oldest son began

running around with a rowdy destructive group of teenagers and was becoming more like them all the time. His wife had for years been gradually withdrawing from him; she insisted on their having separate bedrooms. Finally this man, in his early fifties, had a heart attack.

He was fortunate. He recovered and his near-death was a blessing in disguise. For the first time, he realized the meaning of the gift of life. He understood that there was more to life than overwork: that he had a family, a wife, and a body that would be good to him if he was good to it.

This hard-headed man, who had previously prided himself on how practical he was, began to reform his life. It wasn't easy because he had let things drift so far for such a long time. He began spending time with his wife and children: he gave of himself to make them happy. He worked his 35 or 40 hours a week and did his best. Then, recognizing the transitoriness of human life, he went home and relaxed. The shock of his close call propelled him into efforts to build a happy life day by day. His family, feeling his earnest desire to give, gave back to him and, for the first time, he experienced the thrilling sparks of devoted family life.

He now had work, family, relaxation, hobbies, good sleep, freedom from tension. His wife and he grew back together and his rebellious son received the benefit of his guidance. He was on the road to happiness.

Seven Rules for Happy Living

You can make your life happier and richer. I'm sure these ideas can help you.

1. *Get the happiness habit.* Smile inside, and make this feeling a part of you. Create a happy world for yourself; look forward to each day. Even if some shadows blot out the sunshine, there is always something to feel good about.

2. *Declare war on negative feelings.* Don't let unrealistic worries eat away at you! When negative thoughts invade your mind, fight them. Ask yourself why you, who have every natural right to be happy, must spend your waking hours

wrestling with fear, worry, and hate. Win the war against these insidious twentieth century scourges.

3. *Strengthen your self-image.* See yourself as you've been in your best moments, and give yourself a little appreciation. Visualize your happy times, and the pride you've felt in yourself. Imagine future experiences that will be joyful; give yourself credit for what you are. Stop beating your own brains in!

4. *Learn how to laugh.* Adults sometimes grin or chuckle, but not many can really laugh, I mean a real belly laugh that gives one a sense of release and freedom. Laughing, when it's genuine, is purifying. It is part of your success mechanism, jet-propelling you to victories in life. If you haven't laughed since the age of 10 or 14, go back into the school of your mind and re-learn something you never should have forgotten.

5. *Dig out your buried treasures.* Don't let your talents and resources just die inside you; give them a chance to meet the test of life!

6. *Help others.* Giving to your fellows can be the most rewarding experience of your life. Don't be cynical; understand that many people who seem unpleasant or hostile are wearing a facade that they think will protect them from others. If you give to others, you might be amazed at their grateful, appreciative response. Some people who seem the hardest are really soft and vulnerable. You'll feel great when you can give, without thought of profit.

7. *Seek activities that will make you happy.* Golf, tennis, water skiing? Painting, singing, sewing? I can't tell you—you'll have to tell yourself. But an active life is a happy life, if you're doing what's good for you.

7

Cast Off
Your Emotional Scars

I have been a plastic surgeon for over 25 years and I know just about all there is to know about physical scars. They affect some people intensely, bringing them embarrassment, making them afraid even to examine themselves in the mirror, causing them to retreat from social functions and to encase themselves, hermit-like, in a shell of pain.

Luckily, physical scars can often be removed. I am grateful that my hands have had the power to undo the cruel effects of automobile crashes and other destructive accidents and, in so doing, to restore people's peace of mind. I feel I'm fortunate to be able to render a service to others—it makes me feel good. I feel happy when a patient leaves my office, all smiles, after my operation has corrected a facial scar which was responsible for inner sorrow.

About 10 or 15 years ago, a young actress came to see me. She was a gorgeous girl, and very sweet, but she was in tears over a scar near her nose, the aftermath of one of the holiday weekend statistics you read about in the newspapers every year.

"Don't worry!" I said. "I've seen much worse than that. You'll be fine."

My reassurance did no good. She continued to sob; she was a free spirit and her whole body heaved with the enormity of her grief.

"Here," I said, handing her a mirror, "It's not so bad, is it? And, next time you see me, you'll be as good as new."

She just hung her head and said nothing. Her face to her was her fortune; it meant stage career, meeting a man, marriage.

I operated on her that day. When she returned to my office later that week, I removed the bandages and, when she saw her face, she rushed over to me and kissed me on the cheek. Her face was bright and her heels clicked excitedly as she left to go out into the street—to face life with renewed hope.

Yes, physical scars can be removed.

Emotional Scars Are Painful

But what about emotional scars?

You can't see them—but they can be infinitely painful. You can't feel them—but they can make the stomach rumble and the heart palpitate. There is no evidence of them—but they can cause dizziness, nausea, insomnia, heart attacks, and indigestion.

They are deeper than physical scars and harder to remove. They bring on a vicious cycle of negative feelings which never ends—until you resolve to heal the wound. *But, when you are determined to do this, then you can set about removing the emotional scar.*

Suppose you're a young man in your late twenties. You've had three or four jobs, but you didn't like them and, after a year or so, you gave notice and started looking for greener pastures. Your hunt, however, turned up mostly muddy fields until, one day, you found *the* job. You were hired as assistant personnel director in the offices of a large publishing concern. The director, who hired you, was skeptical of your experience but felt that you might be able to produce what was needed in this job. The salary was good and the prospects of advancement were promising.

There was one catch, however. Most of your experience had been with banks, in a clerical capacity. You needed three or four months to adjust to your new duties. If your boss would be lenient with you, for that period of time, you felt confident that you could make the grade and then your future would be rosy.

The director, an impatient man, afraid of your inexperience, kept an eye on you from the moment you started on the job. You made mistakes, he was critical—and soon you became nervous and committed a number of blunders. One day the director called you in and said he was sorry, but you just weren't suitable for the job.

Since then, you have felt a failure; an emotional scar has taken root within you. You feel resentful. You hate the director, thinking that if he'd only been patient, you would have adjusted to this fine opportunity. You vow that if anyone asks you for a favor—it doesn't matter if it's the loan of fifty cents or help in pushing a car—you will turn him down. You will get even, you tell yourself. If you can't get even with the director, you will take it out on your sister, or the postman, or maybe the cat. Bristling with hostility, you flaunt your emotional scar at the world and the world, reacting with resentment, sets up a nightmarish crosscurrent that seems unending.

How do you heal this emotional scar? You have been treated unfairly, haven't you? What is the answer?

I would say this: You have been treated shabbily and, since this job was important to you, a certain amount of resentment is natural. If you were bitter and short-tempered for a few days after you got notice, this would be understandable. Maybe even desirable, for it is often better to cleanse your system than to let inner hate eat away at you.

But you should not let the scar of resentment take hold of you and permanently dominate your thoughts! There are good things in life, there are other avenues down which you can drive, there are other jobs, other fields. There is a place for you in society if you will meet life halfway.

Forgive the director! You don't know what problems are making him insecure, so that he couldn't give you a fair chance. It took courage for him to hire someone inexperienced in this area. When you made mistakes, he might have been fearful of his responsibility for them.

Forgive because you are a human being too and you're not always fair yourself. Remove the emotional scar and apply yourself to positive goals once again! Get your old perspective back; oil up the old machine and get back on the ball!

To Others, Your Scar Might Seem a Scratch

Your troubles can often seem overwhelming—worse than other people's—to you. But this can work two ways. To others, your scar might seem a scratch.

One man might sulk for years after losing a particular job, but another might shrug it off in 24 hours and go on to a life of success. One girl might resent a lover who married someone else all her life; another girl might buy a new dress, go places with a girl friend and meet another man who is better for her.

If you feel you have the right to be happy, you will not let misfortunes defeat you. You will fight your way through defeats until your life is brighter. You will readjust your aims, realign your compass, set the ship once again on course, and sight future victories.

In *The Power of Your Subsconcious Mind*, Dr. Joseph Murphy writes:

"If you really want peace of mind and inner calm, you will get it. Regardless of how unjustly you have been treated, or how unfair the boss has been, or what a mean scoundrel someone has proved to be, all this makes no difference to you when you awaken to your mental and spiritual powers. You know what you want, and you will definitely refuse to let the thieves (thoughts) of hatred, anger, hostility, and ill will rob you of peace, harmony, health, and happiness. You cease to become upset by people, conditions, news, and events by identifying your thoughts immediately with your aim in life. . . ."

In short, you will recognize that your scar is a scratch. You will wash it with soap, apply iodine or a Bandaid, and go about your job of living zestfully.

You're Tougher than You Think

Some people feel that they've taken too many "hard

knocks" during their lifetime and that these struggles will inevitably take their toll.

This is not so. The human body is a marvelous mechanism and so is the human mind. As a human being, you are truly resilient. You have the bounce of a rubber ball, the drive of a jet engine. You're tough, you can take it—unless you choose to destroy these qualities in yourself.

Franklin D. Roosevelt was struck down by polio, but he did not let it stop him. Most of his adult life he could not walk, being paralyzed, but he carried out the awesome responsibilities of President of the United States without the full use of his limbs.

Helen Keller was totally deaf and blind but she was a strong-minded person and contributed much to the world—as a writer and lecturer and as a cheerful, giving human being who did not waste her time moping over handicaps that would make most people just sit down and cry.

This amazing woman graduated *cum laude* from Radcliffe College and spent her life helping other people who, like herself, were blind and deaf. She wrote articles and books and has traveled all over the world doing work for organizations such as The American Foundation for the Blind.

Walt Disney had his rough times too. In 1931 he had a nervous breakdown. Consummate artist that he was, he could not fully accept his genius at this time in his life. His perfectionism led him to expect too much of himself and he had trouble sleeping. He could not tolerate the imperfections in his productions.

Advised by the studio doctor to leave his work for a while, Disney refused to let his temporary setback crush him. He learned a lesson from it, learned to relax more, and went on to his great career as a cartoon creator and movie maker.

Comedienne Fanny Bryce also had to take it on the chin and bounce back. In *Fabulous Fanny* (Alfred A. Knopf Inc. 1952–53), Norman Katkov tells how crushed "Baby Snooks" was by her divorce in 1927.

"I watched him leave that room," Fanny wrote long years later, "and I didn't believe what was happening. I didn't believe we were through, and I didn't believe I'd never see Nick again as my husband. The lawyer went away to arrange the hotel-room thing, and I knew I was just as much in love with Nick that day as the day I first saw him.

"I waited for Nick to stop the divorce. Even when the lawyer came to take me to court, I thought Nick would be downstairs to call it off. I thought he would be outside the court to stop it. I thought he would be in the court to tell the judge, 'Forget it, Judge, my wife and I made a mistake. We're in love. Why, we don't want a divorce.'

"But he never showed up. All I remember is that it was a beautiful day. I was like in another world. It was like watching me standing there in that courtroom. I didn't hear my lawyer. I didn't hear what the judge said. All I know is they gave me a bunch of papers to sign, and I signed, and they gave me a copy."

Fanny recovered from her hurt to be a great radio and movie comedienne for many years.

These people were tough—and so are you! You have to realize the positive forces that are in you and put them to use, developing faith in yourself as a growing human being who does not knuckle down to a few "bad breaks."

How I Helped a Salesman Conquer His Fears

An insurance salesman came to see me about a year ago. He had read *Psycho-Cybernetics* and he came all the way from Dallas, Texas, for several reasons, one being that he wanted to discuss a problem with me.

He sat opposite me in my living room and, staring unhappily at the carpeting as he talked, told me of his fear of addressing insurance sales meetings in Texas. He was a successful salesman, one of his company's top producers. But when he stood up to address his fellow salesmen, he would panic, mutter a few words and sit down, ashamed of himself. His terror was so great that he would be afraid of fainting.

Sometimes he would take his wife to these meetings and he would be distressed that she should witness his degradation. He would imagine that people in the audience were talking about him, ridiculing him.

I saw before me this middle-aged, good-looking, intelligent man. There was something clean-cut and decent about him and I smoked my cigar and tried to figure out what I could say that would bring him comfort.

"It's strange," I said, "that you, a salesman, who has to make an impression on others, should be afflicted with an imaginary illness."

"It's not imaginary," he answered. "I feel scared."

"It *is* imaginary. You're a good speaker. You're articulate. Yet something happens when you step up to address a group of salesmen in your field.

"Let me tell you a story about myself and then I'll tell you what's wrong with you.

"The whole business of fear can translate itself into many ridiculous patterns that make you much less than what you really are.

"I remember when I was a medical student and in a course on pathology, as the oral examination, the professor would call on me to answer questions. Invariably, I was like you. When I saw the faces of 80 other students staring at me, fear overcame me. I panicked and couldn't think. I would sit down without answering the questions, feeling defeated, because I immediately was able to put my thoughts together and figure out the answer to the questions I had flubbed.

"On written exams I didn't have to face all the students. Looking through the microscope, I wrote down what I saw. Calm, I got *A* on the written exams, but I was afraid I would flunk the course because of the orals and not become a doctor. I was like a poor swimmer who had to make it to shore or drown—I had to master my problem to survive.

"I said to myself that, when called on, I would imagine I was looking through a microscope at slides and this would give me more confidence. Also, I would tell myself that I had a right to make some mistakes and that they shouldn't make me ashamed of myself.

"The next time I stood up and answered the questions. Once, when I hesitated, I told myself that I was only human and I recovered my composure. I passed the course with honors.

"I went through the same pains as you—in a different way, but for the same reason. I was afraid to make a mistake and this fear caused me to lose control of my rational thinking for a moment so I lost the answer.

"My friend, this should be a lesson for you, because your trouble is that you're afraid to make a mistake in the presence of your fellow salesmen. You're emotionally scarred because this fear obsesses you.

"But remember, your colleagues have made mistakes too. And also remember, you've had successes. When you get up to speak next time, think of how you felt last time you sold a big insurance policy. This will give you confidence in yourself and remove the scar.

"The beginning of living is not so much fear, but overcoming the fear of making a mistake. Living begins when we rise above our failures."

The salesman went back to his home in Texas. Since his return, he has been able to address insurance sales groups effectively. His aims remain high, but he is no longer ashamed when he is not perfect. His emotional scar has gone.

You can remove your emotional scars; these two suggestions will help you:

1. Do not try to be someone else.
2. Do not be fearful of making a mistake.

How to Fight Your Way Out of a Depression

Sometimes you will feel depressed. I don't care who you are, now and then your mood will be heavy and you'll think dark thoughts. You'll hate yourself for all the sins of commission and omission that you've ever committed. You will be hard to please and, when you look in the mirror, you won't be fond of what you see.

Many areas of depression stem from maladjustment within the self. If you basically accept yourself, your depressed mood will not last long. Your depressions will be chronic only if you cannot make peace with yourself.

Here's how to fight your way out of a depression:

1. Accept your mood—don't blame yourself for it.
2. Drop your grudges against others; remember that they have problems too.

3. See your past successes and recapture your good feelings about yourself.

Feeling depressed once in a while is not hard to take if you know you can quickly find your way back into the sunshine.

Believe in Yourself and You Won't Be Hurt

Like is like a game of football. You're the quarterback, but sometimes you'll call the wrong plays. You'll send your fullback—also you—straight ahead, one yard to a touchdown, and he'll bump into a wall of tacklers and go nowhere—with only bruises to show for it. Just don't let these bruises become permanent scars that sour you on life and blind you to its moments of beauty.

Psychologists tell us there are "accident-prone" people. When they get tackled hard, they are good bets to get seriously injured.

Others can carry the ball and, when jolted to the ground, get up crisply and run back to the huddle, ready to try again. They believe in themselves and therefore they're not easy to hurt.

Some days will go wrong. The alarm clock won't go off and you'll be late to work, you'll get caught in a rainstorm without an umbrella, your wife will be cranky and the baby will be howling. Your car will need a new repair and you'll wonder how to fit that in the budget; someone will make a mildly sarcastic remark and you'll bark at him as if he had set your house on fire.

You have something to sustain you when irritations pop up—if you believe in yourself. You must be kind to yourself, see yourself as someone who is worthwhile. Instead of harping on your weaknesses, you must see your strengths and picture yourself at your best. You must visualize the you that you like and believe in your positive impulses. If you do, you'll score touchdowns every day. You'll kick extra points too, and you won't get carried off the field on a stretcher.

You Can Shake Off Old Emotional Scars

"But," you may say, "I'm not a youngster in his twenties. I'm 60 and life hasn't been easy. How can I possibly shake off old emotional scars when they've hardened over the years?"

It's not easy. We all wish for a paradise on earth, living on a Polynesian island watching the blue ocean glitter, with coconuts falling off the trees to give us succor. Often we refuse to renounce this dream and, disillusioned, encase ourselves in shells of resentment, thinking of our life full of disappointments and compromises.

But you can get rid of your emotional scars.

Are you a married woman, bitter at your husband because he never could earn enough money to provide you with the material possessions you wanted?

Or a lonely bachelor, still angry at a girl who turned down your marriage proposal almost 30 years ago?

Or a divorced woman, still resentful of your former mate, blaming him for all your troubles?

Or a middle-aged man, a clerk, who feels ashamed that you never climbed higher up the ladder of vocational success?

If you are—or if different emotional ailments plague you—it is time to remove these scars and face life fresh. You can do it if you will surrender your resentment and, like a newborn chicken breaking through its shell, look at a new world which is the only one you've got.

The key to your surgical kit is forgiveness.

Forgive Others—They Are Only Human

Forgive others. Do it not only for their sake, but for your own. If you don't, you will feel within you nauseating resentment, destroying you from within.

Physical scars are not always negative. In some societies, physical scars are signs of prestige. Some natives of Africa disfigure their noses and put rings in them; they then consider themselves beautiful. Creoles in this country used to show off facial scars as symbols of bravery.

But emotional scars always hurt. When you hold a grudge against someone, you may hurt his feelings—but you will harm yourself more.

When someone has done you a real or imagined wrong, an initial angry reaction is natural. Perhaps you should tell the other person how you feel about his action. Steps might then be taken to correct the situation.

If the wrong can't be undone, seething about it for weeks, months, years will not help. The anger will just hurt your stomach and you may end up with ulcers.

Also, remember that the other person is a human being, the same as you, and few of us can say that we have never stepped on another's toes.

So forgive—and forget. Chances are strong that you really have nothing to forgive anyway.

Don't Hold a Grudge against Yourself!

Most important, forgive yourself! You cannot be happy and successful if you hold a grudge against yourself.

Remove your emotional scars with the ointment of kindness. Apply it gently in the area which hurts. If your lifelong fear of romantic entanglements has kept you from marriage, be your own gentle doctor and accept this limitation. If your inability to channelize aggressive forces has kept you from vocational achievements, apply the soothing salve of kind thinking to this wound and rub gently till it no longer hurts. If something you blurted out once hurt a dear friend greatly, be good to yourself and forgive yourself for being human.

Here are four "miracle drugs" for your emotional scars; they've helped others and they'll help you:

1. *Accept your limitations.* No one is perfect; we all have our faults. If you stretch even a rubber band beyond its limits, it will break.

2. *Forget your mistakes.* We've all done things we'd like to undo, but it can't be done. Stop torturing yourself with self-blame!

3. *Forgive others.* They're just as fallible as you are.

They're not gods and they're not machines; they're just *human* beings.

4. *See yourself at your best.* Picture yourself in the situations you've really relished, when things seemed to fit into place and your world was as you like it. Remember how you felt, recapture the good feeling, visualize it in glowing technicolor, and don't be afraid to hold on to this glorious feeling if its impact shocks you. Keep these pleasant images alive in your mind; reject your "failure" images and the sinking feeling in your stomach that goes along with them. Feed your success mechanism!

You can heal your emotional scars with these concepts, enhancing your self-image. Once you begin to like yourself better, undoing the damage of the past, you will be ready to move toward the achievement of successes that are realistic for you and toward the cultivation of constructive habits that lead to happiness.

8

When the Curtain Goes Up,
You Don't Need a Mask

I invite you to relax in the playhouse of your mind and see a drama in which you take part:

It's a masquerade ball at the home of a friend of yours. There's laughter and excited conversation. Everyone wears a mask; you can't even recognize the host, even though you know his face well.

A blonde woman wearing a pink mask says "hello" and you answer her greeting. She's tall and slim, you know her from somewhere—but who is she? A man with cowboy clothes and a black mask takes her arm and leads her over to an improvised dance floor, a space made by pushing back the sofa and the TV set. He's not Tom Mix or the Lone Ranger, but who is he?

It's all very confusing, but it's a game and you're having fun. You drink some punch—"what's in this bowl anyhow?" —and join a laughing group of people. No one takes life seriously for the moment.

Symbolically, this scene is true to life, for most people wear masks almost every day of their lives. You can't see them, but they're there. Our real-life masks are tragic, where the masquerade disguises are amusing. They serve an insidious purpose: to hide your real self, which you feel is unacceptable, from a threatening world.

Many people live their little masquerades till the day they die, putting on the faces they feel will shield them from others' censure. They keep their real selves locked up inside, like some dark secret that terrifies them.

Some people live to ripe old ages without anyone ever really knowing what they're like. Their masks keep them from the imperfect, chaotic give-and-take that is living.

The Masks We All Wear

Are masks necessary?

Our primordial ancestors many centuries ago were savages. When two of them, searching the earth for food, came face to face in an open field, they would both grit their teeth, jut out their lips in defiance and stare at each other menacingly until they finally came to blows. After the fight, the loser would feel fear and might weep unrestrainedly, while the worry on the victor's face would be gone, replaced by the laughter of success. When they met in the future, the beaten man would look fearful, maybe terrified, while the winner would wear the face of confidence.

We, in this civilized society, are also winners and losers, but the picture is grayer. Most of us know the taste of both success and failure and our days may be up and down.

As young children, we are primitive, like our ancestors. If a boy of three takes a bad fall and skins his knee severely, he may howl with pain. If a girl of five receives a pretty birthday present, she may squeal with satisfaction and clap her hands. Most young children express what they feel openly.

In later childhood, in adolescence and as adults, we learn to wear masks, to hide our clean-cut feelings—or to modify them. This is part of the civilizing process; if we would live in a society that can endure, we cannot attack each other physically. We must sometimes put reins on our emotions and the actions which flow from them. We must think of more than our own well-being; our neighbors count too.

In certain situations, we *must* mask our feelings. If you don't like your boss, for example, and you need the money your job brings you to support yourself, a wife, and children —you might have to conceal your dislike to survive.

The trouble is, however, that many people wear masks

when they don't have to. This is over-civilization and it leads to inhibition, confusion and weakening of the person's self-image.

We wear too many masks.

The weak man wears a mask of stoicism that covers up his oversensitiveness to injury.

The vain woman wears a mask of indifference that covers up her desire to be liked.

The man who feels he has failed as a breadwinner may wear the mask of the braggart, boring people with his tall tales of success.

The woman who wants to get married pretends that's the last thing that would ever enter her head.

These are just a few of the many masks we wear. Sometimes they protect you from a snide remark or two, but they also isolate you from contact with the millions of people who appreciate fundamental honesty, a trait that is becoming more and more rare.

Don't Let "Perfection" Frighten You!

Some people retreat into a defensive shell because of their superficial evaluations of other people. Heavily masked people fool them.

Most people who seem perfect frighten others. Their poise is so complete, their appearance so impeccable, and they hide their emotions so flawlessly. Since they appear to be almost inhumanly perfect, they produce inferiority feelings in others, who feel that by comparison they are worthless.

Don't let such pretense frighten you! Recognize it for what it really is: another person's defensive attempt to camouflage his human frailty.

When you see constant perfection in another person, never feel that you must imitate it.

If you can be yourself, with all your human weakness, you're far better off than someone who has to mask himself to stand the strains of modern life.

You Can Be Genuine

It's not always easy to be yourself because your weaknesses would then be open to attack and, realistically, there are always bullies around looking to lift their egos at someone else's expense.

There are some situations in which being yourself, totally unmasked, is unwise. If you're an unconventional person, uninhibited conduct could cost you a job; also, you could undergo a great deal of embarrassment in situations which societal control governs rigidly. You certainly would have the common sense to suppress a whoop of happy laughter during the solemn part of a marriage ceremony, even if your emotion was only a friendly one.

Too many people, however, hide their true selves when such suppression is not necessary. This is something like putting yourself in jail for an offense you haven't even committed.

Some people are afraid that if they're genuine, they'll be censured for being "different." This seems to me an odd criticism since we are all different, and we should be grateful that we are individual. This gives our lives a certain importance they wouldn't have if we were just robots. Yet some of us prefer to play it safe, living like robots and avoiding potential criticism.

This is a terrible sacrifice. Criticism can sting but if you have any kind of belief in yourself, you can take it and if a bully picks on you, you will be able to put him in his place.

You can, and should, be yourself; life offers you many opportunities without punishment or social ostracism. Sometimes you may even be rewarded for your honesty and uniqueness.

In many fields—entertainment is one—there is great demand for people whose performance is of high caliber and therefore different. The most attractive person at a party is often one whose comments are interesting because they are all his own. Many business executives climb the ladder of success not through just conforming, but because they have been willing to gamble on the originality of their creative ideas.

Take a good, long look at your fear of being different and you'll find that much of your fear is groundless.

Over-conformity can take a heavy toll; it can produce unhappiness. Amy Selwyn's article in the April, 1957 *Parents' Magazine,* "Must Your Child Conform," analyzes the effects of overmasking on children:

"Lately psychologists and sociologists have been taking a close look at children's social relationships. Their research shows that children who fit smoothly into the group and pattern their activities to match their friend's are generally more popular and admired. Some of these children are happy and secure, and their compatibility with other children is for them a sign of sound development. But some children who seem outwardly the same are tortured by anxiety and deep emotional problems. For example, ten-year old Joe is the most popular boy in his class. The other children always pick Joe first for a team, a committee, the lead in a class play.

"You might wish that your child were as popular as Joe and fitted as smoothly into his group. But a series of psychological tests showed Joe to be a gravely troubled boy, full of anxiety and fear of failure. He sees himself as unable to cope successfully with life. He doesn't know why he feels this way but thinks that somehow it is all his fault. He has strong feelings of aggression and hostility that he doesn't dare express. It is primarily to cover up his inner anger and guilt that he is friendly and conforms to the other children's expectations."

Popularity often cannot compensate for the self-injury involved in overmasking. Furthermore, in acting out a part, you may end up losing track of who you are.

A Good Friend Will Like You for Yourself

Did you ever hear the story about the fellow who was describing a friend of his? "He's always smiling, always helpful, I've known him 15 years and he's never once lost his temper or even been irritable."

Whereupon his companion sagely remarked, "He sounds like a *saint,* but is he a *friend?*"

106

A good friend will like you for yourself, not for the mask that disguises who you are.

On Halloween young friends band together, don masks and prepare for a day of doorbell-ringing and fun. Masks and Halloween spell gaiety.

For adults, however, forgetting such festive occasions, built-in masks generally spell tragedy. They point to friendships built out of paper, not granite. They mean hiding, not giving.

If you feel that you must conceal your real personality from a friend, then one of you is not a good friend. A real friend will accept you as you are, with your strengths and weaknesses, mistakes and victories. The marriage vow, made "for better or for worse," binds two friends who, ideally, get to know each other in all moods and situations, with disguise impossible, and accept each other, ignoring imperfections.

A good friendship will be like this. You and your friend will know each other—unmasked—and will be loyal to each other's interests.

How a Schoolteacher Moved Toward Freedom

Five or ten years ago, a schoolteacher came to my office. She was unhappy with her face. No feature pleased her. Her nose was too long, her chin too weak, her ears stood out—or so she thought.

I looked at her. I had never seen her before and felt that my appraisal was quite objective. I saw that she was not a bad-looking woman, that her trouble was her poor estimate of herself.

I improved her appearance with some minor plastic surgery, less than she thought she needed; as I got to know her, I observed that her manner was extremely guarded. She rarely showed even the mildest emotion on her face.

"That's all I can do for you as a plastic surgeon," I said.

She seemed annoyed, but her voice was perfectly modulated as she studied herself in the mirror. "You didn't change my face very much," she accused.

I decided to be completely frank. "Only a little work was

needed. I did it, and there's now nothing at all wrong with your face. It's the way you use it—as a mask to cover your feelings."

She looked hurt; her head drooped. "I do my best."

"I'm sure you do," I said. "But, tell me, do you over-control yourself as a teacher?"

Sensing that I was sincere in my desire to help her, she slowly let her defenses down and told me about the miseries in her life. She hated teaching, feeling that she had to be a perfect example for her pupils. Every day she would go to school wearing her imprisoning mask, a model of propriety, hiding all feelings except what she felt to be the "correct" ones. She had always been reserved; now, after three years of teaching, she felt unbearably tense. Not knowing what the trouble was, she misplaced it onto her facial features.

She concluded her story, then burst out weeping. "The kids laugh at me," she sobbed. She stopped suddenly, blew her nose and sat erect in her chair, looking at me guardedly as if she'd let a horrible secret out.

I smiled. "That's better," I said. "Crying shows that you're human, that you have feelings."

Slowly she relaxed and smiled back.

"The kids laugh at you," I said, "because they can feel that you're always acting, always put on. As a teacher, of course you have to have self-control. You have to appear competent and mature. But—you don't have to be perfect. A good teacher can look foolish once in a while and her pupils will still respect her if she's basically sound—they'll like her for being human. Get rid of your mask! You'll feel better with yourself, and you might even enjoy teaching."

She felt better when she left my office, resolving to be a freer person. A few months later, she wrote me that she no longer worried about her face, that she felt more relaxed. She felt that she was a more human teacher and, while she still had anxieties in her job, she was confident that in time her classroom would cease to be her jail.

Unlocking the Door to Your Real Self-Image

Learn a lesson from this story; let it help you. Your self-image will be strong only when you unlock the door to your human feelings—and failings. Otherwise, you will be masked, like a criminal about to break into a bank.

Assuming that you are not a bank robber, you have no need for a mask—not basically, anyway. Your feelings are not so dreadful that you need to inhibit them constantly. If you think they are, it is your thinking that needs revision, not your feelings.

If you bury your feelings deep inside you, you cannot have an accurate self-image, because you cannot possibly know what you're really like. You can only know what you're pretending to be.

If you're at a party, explaining a heartfelt idea to some people and they frown, do you stop talking or change the subject? You must develop the power of your own convictions and stop looking to others for approval or recognition. Otherwise you will choke off your self-expression and hide behind a mask, crushing your creative self.

Many people were squelched as children and have come to feel that they are unimportant. They constantly take a back seat to others, feeling they are failures and suffering from a deep sense of inferiority.

If this describes you, bury the past and throw off your wraps! Assert your right to be an individual! Be a good parent to yourself; throw off the chains of over-caution and unlock the door to a self-image that has room to expand!

The Secret of Personality

Much has been written about "personality," which *Webster's Dictionary* defines as the "quality or state of being personal, or of being a person."

Some writers tell you that to have "personality," you should be dynamic, or learn some social skills, or talk about interesting experiences you've had.

I'm against none of these things, but I feel that their approach to the subject is superficial. To have "personality," to have "the quality of being a person," you must be able to shed your mask and be yourself, not someone acting out a part in a play which he hasn't written or even helped create.

The great secret of personality is that *you must learn to throw away your mask and be yourself.*

These concepts can help you:

1. *Do not be afraid to be different.* The people who will scoff at you for your uniqueness are beneath your attention; our greatest creative minds and practical leaders are not afraid to be different; if they were, they wouldn't have reached their levels of success.

2. *Lose your fear of "perfect people."* They are not perfect; they are only acting a part. Don't compare yourself unfavorably to such "paragons of perfection!"

3. *Try to be more spontaneous.* Learn to let go a little. When you're about to talk, don't prepare beforehand what you will say; let the words come out! Most people hate to listen to "canned" conversation; they don't trust it. Remember this: if you say something that sounds silly, nobody's going to shoot you for it. You'll still be alive and it won't be the last time that you'll be imperfect—at least I hope not.

4. *Rely on yourself.* A mature person accepts himself, does not look to others for approval. A storyteller who looks from face to face for a smile as he tells a joke will probably end up with no audience. People like to be entertained, dislike being forced to respond. If you look on your own actions with kindness, you will be able to express yourself freely.

5. *Squelch your self-critical thoughts.* If you keep criticizing yourself, you will crush your courageous impulses. When you tell yourself, "Maybe I'm foolish" or "Perhaps I'm too assertive" or "I shouldn't have talked so fast," you destroy your real personality and you're liable to hurriedly get a mask on your face, feeling almost hysterical. Declare war on your self-critical thoughts! Stop tormenting yourself!

6. *Shed your mantle of dignity.* Too many people feel they must be dignified, that it is not proper to express enthusiasm. This is ridiculous. A full person should be able to express indignation and, even more, to express positive feelings such as love and enthusiasm. If a friend does you a good turn, don't feel it's shameful to say, "Joe, that was wonder-

ful of you!" And, if your wife looks beautiful, don't just nod your head quietly. Put your arms around her and tell her she looks gorgeous. You'll enjoy the wonderful feeling that you can make others happy, and they will like to be with you.

A word of caution, once again: In some situations, you must realistically inhibit yourself. If you have a new job or a new boss, and you're working in a very conventional setting, it might be wise to be cautious. But don't overdo the restraint! And, in even such a situation, there may be more freedom for you than you might think.

Practice Exercise No. 5: Be Yourself

Let's get back to one of the wonderful tools you have at your command—your imagination.

Sit in a quiet place where you can concentrate on the job of unmasking yourself and being yourself—without camouflage and pretense. Quiet down your thoughts, wrestle away your worries, and just relax.

Now call on your imagination to project you into the future. Set a goal for yourself, the achievement of which would make you happy, and picture the steps you will take. Mentally image the situations you'll be involved in, see them in concrete detail.

As you move toward your goal, you will make clever moves and yet sometimes you will stumble and fall flat on your face. Here's the main point of this exercise: As your mental pictures weave in your mind, *accept your mistakes as well as your winning ways*. To be realistic about yourself, and have the ability to be yourself without a mask, *you must be willing to examine and accept your failings*.

Needless to say, your aim is self-improvement, not the encouragement of error. But you must always have a bottom under you, to give you support when things go wrong. If you have no such support, then you'll have to wear a mask.

Let's take an example. You're trying something new. You're a widow, your husband having died two years before. Since his death, you've kept to yourself, feeling sad and lonely. Now you feel a desire to have some people over to your house; you invite them over.

It's a new experience—your husband used to help you as co-host—and you feel anxious. You're afraid you might push people to talk in a ridiculous way or maybe you'll tell a story and forget the punchline. Well, you might. Here's the main point: *If you do, and you still accept yourself, you have a floor under you and you have nothing to fear.* You have no need to wear a mask!

This is just an example of what I mean. Naturally, each of you will have your own dreams, your own specific situations, your own problems.

In the sanctuary of your mind, picture your goal and move toward it step by step. Then, as you imagine your erring, see and feel the embarrassment of it; but also see yourself accepting your lack of perfection, living with it, giving yourself understanding when you need it.

This exercise will help you to be yourself for, if you can live with your mistakes, you will never hide behind a mask.

9

Sex and the Self-Image

Sex is much talked about—in public and in private. It used to be a taboo subject, when I was a boy, but today almost everybody talks about it. In pre-Freudian days, people would blush at the mention of this "sinful" word; today it is a fashionable word. In a way, this is healthy, for it is harmful to hide anything important in darkness.

And yet, with all the fuss, *many people talk about sex with such ignorance.*

You've all stopped at a newsstand and glanced around you —at endless magazine covers of bosomy blondes trying to entice you; at paperback book covers of muscular "he-men" attacking half-naked, curvy girls; at newspaper headlines screaming of sexual attack in large, black type.

Is this what sex is all about? Is sex a woman with 38-size bosom and perfect legs? Is sex a man six-foot tall with bulging muscles?

Remember the old proverb: *You can't judge a book by its cover?* Well, it's that way with sex! And men who are five foot two can take comfort. So can women who are some-what tall or overweight by current beauty standards. For sex is not just something physical. You can't order it at your department store and you can't buy it, all packaged, at your supermarket.

Sex is spiritual, sex is something that is in your heart and soul.

The Hollywood Sex Image

Where did all the trouble start? When did sex become a commodity? I'm not a sociologist or a sexologist, so I can't give you a definite answer.

But probably the development of the motion picture industry had something to do with it. As the popularity of movies became a national institution, people began to hero-worship beautiful (or handsome) Hollywood stars, and these stars became symbols of desirability. Movies being a visual communications medium, the emphasis was on the image and physical appearance became of paramount importance.

Adolescent boys and girls, forming their own self-images, tried to model themselves after reigning movie queens and kings, but often this imitation was superficial and hollow— as much so as many of the unrealistic motion pictures that have come off the production lines.

And so, too often today, grownups—who were once adolescents—model their sexual self-image after the concepts they have learned watching Hollywood movies.

But sexual appeal is much more than a physical thing. Good looks are nice, but they are secondary to spiritual substance and emotional maturity.

The Homely Boy Who Got the Dance with the Pretty Girl

Believe me, I am telling you the truth. But do more than this: *visualize it!* Go back into the theatre of your mind. Sit down in your chair, munch some popcorn if you wish, and enjoy the drama which I will unfold for you. The plot is real; this is not an unrealistic soap opera.

There's a school dance in this large gymnasium. The 14-piece orchestra is playing and the dance floor is crowded. The boys are wearing suits, ties and white shirts. The girls are wearing pretty red and blue and black dresses, their hair is pretty and they wear high heels. There's laughter and conversation as people enjoy themselves or try to pretend they're having fun.

On the sidelines many teenagers stand in groups. Three girls are standing together giggling and nearby are six boys, trying to look sophisticated and confident. A tall, handsome young man leaves his group, walks smoothly up to one of the girls, an attractive redhead in a green dress, and asks her for the next dance.

"Sorry, Jim, but all my dances are booked up."

The boy's chin drops and he mutters something and goes back to his group. "I'm a jerk," he snarls. "Why did I even ask her? Who does she think she is?"

The other guys kid him. Then one fellow, not so good-looking, a head shorter, too skinny, says, "Well, I'd like to ask her."

The tall, good-looking fellow says, "Come on. She wouldn't dance with you—not in a million years."

The shorter fellow smiles agreeably, walks over to the girl, she nods at him and they walk over to the dance floor and begin foxtrotting.

Later, there's an intermission and, while the orchestra takes a break, Harriet and her girl friend Geraldine drink punch at the refreshment table. Harriet says, "You know, Jeri, I couldn't help hearing the boys talking to Jim a few minutes ago. He's sore because you turned him down."

"Jim? Who does he think he is? What a conceited nothing! He has looks, sure, but he's too aggressive and overbearing. He thinks he's God's gift to women. He can fool some girls, but not me.

"Now Steve, he's short, but I like him. He has a wonderful sense of humor and he's just himself—he doesn't try to impress me or to be someone else. He's friendly and considerate and he doesn't think he's doing me a favor by asking me to dance."

All right, you have seen this drama. Learn from it!

Is Sex Skin-Deep?

Learn that sex appeal is not good looks. It is not "glamorous" clothes. It is not a smooth manner.

If your success mechanism works for you, if you feel that

men are your brothers and women are your sisters, if you feel part of humanity, if you're willing to bend if you make a mistake, if you're not afraid to love somebody—then you're on first base sexually.

If you care about people, if you are capable of feeling compassion, these qualities contribute to your sexual attraction. If you have a sense of direction and if you are capable of understanding another's needs, if you have self-confidence and accept yourself as you are, these qualities also enhance your sexual appeal. These qualities are basic to the appeal of a woman as well at that of a man. In my drama, Jeri chose Steve over Jim because he was a well-rounded person whom she liked. Jim's negative character traits took away from his physical attractiveness. Steve, on the other hand, was a charitable person.

By "charitable" I don't mean that one gives large financial contributions to the Community Chest or the Red Cross. A charitable person is sympathetic to people and understands his role in the world, knows that he will get what he gives. Steve's attraction was his outgoing personality which gave to others. Jim was narcissistic, felt only for himself, and thought that was enough.

A woman, whether she's 18 or 60, without knowing it, looks for this consideration in a man. One reason why the newspapers are full of stories about Hollywood stars leaving young musclemen is that so often she discovers that's all the guy has—muscles. The more mature a girl is, the more she will go toward men with strong emotional qualities.

Provided that a woman is not extremely ugly, a sensible man will also go toward her if she is emotionally mature. As a young man, he may be attracted mostly to physical qualities, but when he wants to get married and settle down, he will—if he's wise—look for a woman with heart. Famous men often choose to marry normal, average women who are considerate and comfortable to live with.

This doesn't mean that beautiful women are just nothings. More and more, they realize that more is needed than beauty.

But some beautiful women are spoiled. Used to taking, not giving, some expect the world to be handed to them on a platter. They are heading for heartache and, when they get older and their physical beauty fades, they feel that they have lost everything.

The physical aspect does exist, though, in sex, and an ugly deformity brings suffering. Literature is full of deformed people who come to tragic ends. There's the classic case of the "Hunchback of Notre Dame" and the pitiful story of Toulouse-Lautrec, who felt that only a prostitute could tolerate him. In these cases, personal appearance has a deep meaning.

The millions and millions of dollars that women spend each year on cosmetics and hairdressing—this too has meaning. They are not just throwing their money away. Such care for one's physical appearance is healthy. A woman is unhealthy, however, when her looks become primary to her and she overlooks the existence of deeper qualities. Hiding behind a wig, a woman may hide her self-image.

Still, a woman likes to see a good-looking man and a man likes to see a pretty woman. Real ugliness can be a deterrent to sexual appeal.

The "Ugliest Girl in America"

This reminds me of a story.

About 20 years ago, a magazine decided that, instead of looking for the most beautiful girl in America, it would run a contest to choose the ugliest girl in the country. Its motives were not cruel; perhaps, it was felt, this girl could be transformed into a physically desirable girl. The magazine would be doing something positive in staging this contest. This girl would be given a chance to improve herself.

The magazine was flooded with photos from all over the country and the editors picked the "winner," a girl with poor features, terrible grooming, and appalling clothes.

Her fare was paid to New York and specialists went to work on her. I was called in to fix her nose and build up her chin, a hairdresser improved her hairdo, clothes experts fitted her out with new dresses and hats, and a few other technicians did their part. And she became stunning almost overnight!

To cap this amazing Cinderella story, a few months later she was married. I heard about her a few years ago. She has five or six children, if I remember correctly, and I believe she's now a grandmother. Her change in physical appearance brought meaning to her life.

This makes me wonder. Suppose she had never been selected? What would have happened to her? Would she have gotten married? I don't know, but I doubt it. Surely her improved looks helped her chances.

Before the change, she was inhibited. After, she was able to give of herself to others—and she met her husband. This is a success story and it should be a lesson to anyone whose physical appearance is holding her (or him) back. It is true that she received an extraordinary amount of help but, without this aid, you too can better your appearance if it's poor, *if* you're willing to drive yourself into action.

And good physical appearance, along with other aspects of the success mechanism—understanding, compassion, sense of direction, charity, self-esteem and self-acceptance—will improve your self-image and your chances to achieve a good sexual adjustment.

The Truth about Sex

Still, people today are very conscious of appearance; almost everyone makes the most of their natural equipment—physically. Most women especially are neat and trim, well dressed and well groomed.

So that if there is trouble with sex today in spite of all the boastful talk—and I certainly feel there is—it lies in the fact that many people feel it is a *purely physical* thing. The real truth about sex is a glorious one experienced by only a lucky few.

Studies reveal that many of the students in U.S. colleges have inferiority feelings and surely their concepts of themselves are largely concerned with sex, these being young people in their late teens and early twenties.

These are also times of troubled marriages and frequent divorces. Moreover, many people fear marriage too much to undertake such a "traumatic" enterprise and spend their lives in constant, superficial dating, going from summer resort to summer resort, and from dancehall to dancehall. This social treadmill is great for a young man of 25, but is not nearly as appropriate when he's 45 and is still afraid of a deep, basic relationship.

Studies on sexual adjustment in marriage have revealed the existing difficulties. In one study, only slightly more than half of the people interviewed believed there had been a good sexual adjustment from the beginning of the marriage and 12 per cent believed they had never succeeded, even after being married for two decades.

In a survey of 1000 marriages, it was found that two out of every five people were sexually maladjusted.

In another study, almost half the married people interviewed cited sexual maladjustment as the chief trouble in their union.

The case of Marilyn Monroe, one of this century's great "sex symbols," was an especially tragic one. With all her beauty, she thought she lacked something and was lonely in her heart. Gorgeous as she was, her concept of herself was a negative one. It has not, to my knowledge, been conclusively proved that she killed herself but if she did, it is because she thought she was of little value as a person.

I met Marilyn Monroe once on the west coast when she was married to Arthur Miller. I also met her at Sardi's in New York, when we were both dining with the same group. I thought to myself that she was an interesting, alive, intelligent woman. Her opinions were sincere and serious. She seemed charming to me.

But her own self-image was apparently weak and the opinions of others could not change this.

It is ironic that motion picture publicity developed the great image of Marilyn Monroe for millions to see—one of the celebrated sex images of our time—and yet her own self-image was neglected. Today she is dead, a tragic heroine, so people throw bouquets, as they sometimes did when she was living and seemed burdened with a personal guilt stemming from an unhappy childhood. When one's self-image is poor, it is not easy to live with oneself.

And so others gave her a stature which she apparently could not give herself!

This reminds me of something that happened to me a few months ago. My nurse told me that a woman wanted to see me. She had read my books and knew a friend of mine, and she wanted to tell me her troubles. I'm not a psychiatrist, but I said I'd be happy to listen to her if it would help ease her mind.

She had been raped by a soldier in a small town when she was just four years old and later, at ten, her father had made sexual advances. She seemed relieved to tell me about these sordid childhood experiences and to feel that I still accepted her.

I saw before me a good-looking middle-aged woman, intelligent and sensitive, but I could also sense that she did not feel her own worth. This blot from the past still infected her soul and she had no proper focus on the fine qualities she really possessed. I doubt that she emotionally felt herself worthy of enjoying a full sexual experience with her husband.

Sex appeal—real sex appeal—is accentuating the positive and eliminating the negative. It is overcoming your failure instincts and relying on your success mechanism.

Fear, anger, uncertainty are feelings which make people withdraw from other people into a world of emptiness. To attain real sex appeal, you must lick these negative feelings and live dynamically and positively.

The sex act itself is more than a physical act. It involves true participation, and unreserved giving between two people.

Masculinity and Femininity

There is much talk these days about "masculinity" and "femininity." What should a man be like and what should a woman be like?

I feel that this is another little-understood subject. There are men and there are men; there are women and there are women. All are unique. God created all to be themselves, not to be governed by rigidly prescribed rules.

This is another area of illusion in these troubled times. If you see a tall, hairy, handsome young man in a television commercial, and he looks vigorous and athletic, is he more "masculine" than, say, Albert Schweitzer, who has dedicated himself to humanity?

Curiously, some people would say he is. They would fall once again for the physical image and forget about the heart that gives and the mind that makes us what we are.

It is the Schweitzers of this world who give of themselves to other people and *this, I believe, is a man.* I don't know how tall he is or how muscular, perhaps he is physically strong and perhaps he is not, but this is a man.

Dorothy Dohen, in *Women in Wonderland* (Sheed & Ward, 1960), describes sociologist Margaret Mead's research on males and females in primitive tribes. She studied the customs of the Arapesh, Mundugumor and Tchambuli tribes. "Among the Arapesh she found both sexes gentle, responsive, unaggressive and 'maternal,' both men and women participating in child care; among the Mundugumor, both men and women are aggressive, harsh and violent; among the Tchambuli, sharply divergent roles are prescribed for the sexes and are accompanied by marked temperamental differences, but the roles reverse Western notions about what is naturally male and female; economic life is supervised by the women and the men devote themselves to art and ceremony.

"Margaret Mead's research seemed to prove once and for all that biology is not determining and that it is culture which accounts for the different personalities of men and women," the author concludes.

So you see that different societies have different standards for men and women. In our society, dominated as it is by advertising media and motion pictures, the masculine ideal is the strong, young muscleman with flashing teeth and the feminine ideal is the shapely, bosomy blonde with the perfect legs and the come-on manner.

I cannot fall for this nonsense. To me, a man is biologically a man and a woman is biologically a woman and the physical characteristics take care of themselves. I look for the person. I look for such qualities as compassion and relatedness and self-respect. If a man treats other human beings with the compassion he would have for a loved brother, I say that he is a good man. If he relates to other people simply and sincerely, I say that he is a good man. If he has self-respect, if his self-image is an asset, he is truly complete.

I would judge a woman by the same standards.

Let me say to you reading this book: Do not worry about being "masculine" or "feminine." Just insist upon your right to be yourself, to live as creatively and happily as you can, and to enjoy dynamic give-and-take with your fellow human brothers and sisters.

You Don't Have to Be a Superman

Many of you have doubtless seen the movie "Period of Adjustment," adapted from Tennessee Williams' play. One of the main characters in this comedy is a young man who feels he must be a "superman." As a result, he develops the "shakes," is hospitalized and, when married, gets into all kinds of fights with his wife because he must keep proving what a great, big man he is.

He is all around you. So many men today feel that they must be all-powerful, immune to hurt, stoical. They imprison their soft feelings, crush other people to prove they're men and make life—which, God knows, is difficult enough—just a little harder for other people. And, they torture themselves if they're not just as brave as a private eye they've seen on TV or a cowboy they've seen in a Hollywood movie.

If you, reading this book, feel like this, let me help you relax and enjoy yourself . . . please. It's so simple! Just remember that you were once a little boy who cried when he skinned his knee. Just remember that you're a man and you don't have to prove it all the time, sexually or any other way. Just stop trying to be a superman. You'll feel so much better.

You're as Beautiful as You Feel

And you women, be yourselves! You don't have to look like Lana Turner or Sophia Loren, you don't have to have a perfect figure, and you don't have to act sophisticated or phony. If you're neat and make the most of your physical traits, if you're genuine, if you do your best to fulfill your responsibilities, you'll get along. And, if you feel sisterly compassion for others, people will love you for it.

Remember this absolute truth: If you feel beautiful, you are beautiful, and no one can take it away from you unless you renounce the power of your own happy feelings.

Sex and Marriage

Sex is a simple animal function, and yet it can be giving on the deepest level between two people. In marriage it helps to unite two people who have chosen to merge their destinies.

If two people are able to give to each other, in the partnership of marriage they are able to reinforce each other's strength and encourage each other's individual talents and resources. Through the God-given sexual function, they are able to produce children who are the fruit of their own joy.

If these married people accept each other as they are, without fault-finding, and if they want to be happy and successful, sex will be no problem. It will need no effort, no advice, no learned study.

Marriages are in trouble when people cannot give to each other. A marriage is a complex social relationship, with endless functions and responsibilities involved, especially where there are children. When there's dissension, it can go downhill fast. A house divided against itself will have a hard time surviving.

If two people really care for each other and are willing to forget their grudges after a fight, their marriage can bring them closer to each other and to the rest of the human race. Love is the basic ingredient of a good marriage.

When the children grow up and leave, happily married people will not be desolate, for they still have an affectionate feeling for each other.

If You Love, You Are Someone

Everyone wants to be important; I guess it's a universal desire to want to be "someone." But you don't have to be a millionaire, you don't have to be elected to public office, you don't have to be glamorous or muscular, you don't have to be a war hero! If you love, you are someone!

If you care for other people and do your best to be a contributing member of society, if your liking shines through other people's mistakes and weaknesses—even their occasional hypocrisy—you are someone and people will give you recognition for something that is increasingly becoming all too rare in this world.

As the great English poet Spenser wrote many years ago:

Love is lord of truth and loyalty.

Some day people will stop talking about sex and go back to talking about love.

Giving Will Enhance Your Self-Image

For it is love that involves giving, practicing the qualities that lead to success and inhibiting those that breed failure. Giving to others without idealizing them helps you to accept yourself for what you are, giving true dimension to your self-image. It involves reaching out toward other people, and living more fully.

Psychologist Erich Fromm has expressed this beautifully in *The Art of Loving* (Harper & Row, 1956):

"The most fundamental kind of love, which underlies all types of love, is *brotherly love*. By this I mean the sense of responsibility, care, respect, knowledge of any other human being, the wish to further his life. This is the kind of love the Bible speaks of when it says: love thy neighbor as thyself. Brotherly love is love for all human beings; it is characterized by its very lack of exclusiveness. If I have developed the capacity for love, then I cannot help loving my brothers. In brotherly love there is the experience of union with all men, of human solidarity. Brotherly love is based on the experience that we all are one. The differences in talents, intelligence, knowledge are negligible in comparison with the identity of the human core common to all men. In order to experience this identity it is necessary to penetrate from the periphery to the core. If I perceive in another person mainly the surface, I perceive mainly the differences, that which separates us. If I penetrate to the core, I perceive our identity, the fact of our brotherhood. . . ."

It is this quality of brotherly love which can enable you to communicate fully with the people in your world. Without this ability, you would be separate and fearful and you would be forced either to withdraw from life or to distort its true value. Your self-image can thrive on identification with other people and compassion for their needs, since this helps you to better accept your own problems and appreciate your own virtues.

We are our brother's keepers. God meant it so. Too often we forget this, being embroiled in the dog-eat-dog competitiveness of modern civilization. But actually, when we love others, we are closer to ourselves and to a healthy self-image.

Sex in marriage should represent the height of spiritual and physical giving. Two people ideally give to each other as Nature intended, insuring the propagation of the species—the continuation of life.

Too few people relate this way. A good percentage of the population does not get married, and many marriages end in difficulty or divorce. Deep friendship is not common.

If you have not achieved a feeling of closeness with the opposite sex, do not feel that it is beyond you. You can, with effort, if you'll change your self-image.

If you feel worthless, you have to see new truths about yourself. Otherwise, you'll never go out toward others. You'll figure it's safer to hide behind a shell of inhibitions, as did the "ugliest girl in America" before her physical change.

There are beautiful truths about each of us—if we dehypnotize ourselves from ingrained, negative concepts. Give yourself a break! See yourself at your best, work at developing your most constructive abilities, imagine the triumphs that lie ahead, and work to make these mind pictures a reality.

Relax with a self-image that you're proud of and take a crack at success and happiness! Go back to the practice exercises at the end of many chapters in this book and work on these exercises. Do more than that—think about these ideas and understand how you can make a happy, successful little world for a self that you like.

If you're at peace with your self-image, you'll be able to give to others and will have an excellent chance to consummate a deep sexual relationship, in marriage, which will have real meaning.

10

Accept Your Weakness
and You'll Be Strong

Charity begins at home. You can't be compassionate to others at the same time that you're cruel to yourself. If you are, your compassion will not be completely genuine; you will feel envious when you are giving something to others that you cannot give yourself. It's something like a poor, struggling man finding ten dollars in the gutter and giving it all to a hard-pressed friend of his. How can he help but begrudge his generous gift?

Yet many of you are cruel to yourself. You are critical and condemning of yourself. When you take part in a discussion, you don't like your contribution. When you look at yourself in the mirror, you don't like what you see. When you survey your life, you are dissatisfied with your achievements. You tell yourself that you are weak and you hate yourself for it. *The truth is that you are weak and so am I.* And it's not such a terrible thing!

"Stronger by weakness wiser men become," wrote Edmund Waller, 17th century English poet, and his words ring true today.

We are not supermen and we are not automatons; we are not gods and we are not machines. We are all human beings and the offspring of parents who were human beings. We are products of error and creatures of error. Living in troubled times, we all have moments of despair.

In the words of Erich Fromm *(The Art of Loving)*, "Man is gifted with reason; he is *life being aware of itself;* he has awareness of himself, of his fellow man, of his past, and of the possibilities of his future. This awareness of himself as a separate entity, the awareness of his own short life span, of the fact that without his will he is born and against his will he dies, that he will die before those whom he loves, or they before him, the awareness of his aloneness and separateness, of his helplessness before the forces of nature and of society, all this makes his separate, disunited existence an unbearable prison. He would become insane could he not liberate himself from this prison and reach out, unite himself in some form or other with men, with the world outside."

Yes, man has needs and terrors. But weakness is not a horrible thing, it is not a curse at all—if you accept it.

What Do You Expect of Yourself?

The trouble starts when you hate yourself for your weakness. It is this self-hate that destroys you from the inside, that defeats you before you can get off the ground. Your expectations of yourself are unfair.

If you own an automobile, are you satisfied if it drives smoothly at 50 miles an hour for 350 miles—or do you expect it to rise off the ground and fly?

If you have a dog, are you happy if it's affectionate and comfortable—or do you resent it because it doesn't speak English?

These questions are of course ridiculous, but they point up the absurdity of your expectations of yourself.

Remember this: *The more you accept yourself as you are, with your weaknesses, the better you will be able to function despite the stresses and strains of civilized living.*

You've all heard the "funny" stories of patients in mental institutions who thought they were Napoleon. Poor, suffering souls! They could not accept the mistakes and failures that were part of their lives and, miserable with loathing for themselves, had to live in a make-believe world where they were all-powerful—like Napoleon. They expected so much of themselves that they destroyed their sense of reality and their connection with the world around them.

If you're a baseball fan, you'll recognize these illustrations of this inherent truth. How many times have major league teams signed bonus players for huge sums of money only to see them fail, probably crushed by the pressure of others' great expectations of their performance, while unsung players have quietly moved up through the minor leagues, learning their trade, to major league stardom!

To feel secure, you must raise the ceiling so that you can rise to the heights—but keep a floor below you so you don't fall too far.

The "Tough Guy"

Most American men expect themselves to be tough and stoical. If they fall below certain superficial standards of "toughness," they condemn themselves and crawl into shells of fear and resentment. This can be carried to fantastic extremes. I know men, talented and decent human beings, who have achieved wonderful things in their lives, who are afraid of the slightest suggestion that they are not "tough guys" too.

Isn't this silly? Yet this "tough guy" fabric has taken root among men in our culture. I wouldn't be surprised if some men who have committed suicide have done this dreadful act out of self-hatred, arising from their inability to accept weaknesses in themselves, normal weaknesses which most human beings share.

I know men who thought of armed combat during World War II not as an unavoidable duty, but as an enjoyable opportunity to prove their courage. They were not sadists, nor were they blind to the very real dangers of death or crippling. Their desire to prove to themselves and the world that they were "tough" was so strong that no other considerations ever existed.

The August 3, 1963, issue of *TV Guide* contains an interesting article about Skitch Henderson, the talented musical conductor of TV's *Tonight* show. ("Skitch Henderson," by Maurice Zolotow.)

". . . His mother and father had one of those agonizing marriages which resulted in divorce when he was very young. Then his mother died. . . .

"He was abnormally underweight and oversensitive as a boy. He was a physical coward. . . .

"He was constantly being beaten up and ridiculed. His male identity was so threatened that when he grew up, he was constantly risking his life to prove he was not afraid to die—racing on the official team of the Mercedes-Benz company, slaloming down the steepest slopes of Sugarbush, Vermont, volunteering for the Army Air Force during World War II.

"He flew the P-38 Lightning with the 15th, 9th and 4th divisions of the U.S. Air Force in the Pacific. He still holds the rank of major in the aviation reserve. Whenever reporting for his annual service, he flew a jet. . . . He has the kind of raw guts that one does not normally associate with a musician.

"He didn't want to be a musician, really, but it was the one way he had of establishing anything real about himself."

This story is instructive. Here is Skitch Henderson, a man who is charming, talented and extremely successful in his field, a man of outstanding sensitivity—and yet he, too, seemed to fall for the American "tough guy" myth, risking his life to prove himself.

Millions of you American men are in this boat, with a Captain Bligh-like, slave-driving master egging you on. You may think the pursuit is worthwhile, but it will lead you only to high-blood pressure and a shattered self-image.

A noted psychologist recently blamed the "suicidal cult of manliness" for the fact that, in American society, men seem to lack women's longevity. Many a man would rather switch the old saying around and be a "dead hero" rather than a "live coward."

Actually, though, it's not a question of either heroism or cowardice; we're talking about a common sense approach to a man's simple self-acceptance, as opposed to the artificial ideal of the "tough guy." We're trying to recognize that every man is not 100% "he-man" nor should anyone expect him to be like this.

One of the most intelligent analyses of the subject is in Dr. David Abrahamsen's *The Road to Emotional Maturity*:

"In reality, we are all a *mixture* of masculine and feminine traits. Although this mixture is at the root of many of your personality upsets, *it can also be one of your most valuable allies in helping you to cope with many of your daily problems*. On your road to achieving emotional maturity you can utilize your knowledge about your male and female characteristics in a way that is beneficial to your emotional development. . . .

"Generally, as we grow up, we are taught to consider certain personality traits as either masculine or feminine. For instance, a man is *supposed* to be hard and unemotional; and a woman *should* be tender and sympathetic. When he is little, a boy is expected to want to run out to play ball with the boys all the time; a girl is expected to want to sit home and play with her dolls. If, as happens in many cases, the boy prefers to sit home and read, or listen to music, or do something by himself, he is called a 'sissy,' meaning that he has feminine traits. If the girl prefers to play ball, she is considered a tomboy. In a like manner, the man is *expected* to be independent, and the woman is *expected* to be dependent—she should not *want* a career; a man should be domineering and a woman *should* be submissive; he serious, she flirtatious; he logical, she intuitive. We can see how a conflict begins to arise, because men and women just don't fall into a pattern of either all masculine or all feminine traits—but they feel that they are expected to.

"What really is femininity and masculinity? You may wonder at this point, for we have described the traits which are generally considered feminine or masculine. *Femininity, we may say, means that a person prefers a passive goal to an active goal. . . . Masculinity, we may say, means that a person prefers an active goal to a passive one. . . .*"

A man does not have to be "tough" all the time. Does it make you more of a man if you talk out of the side of your mouth, like a Prohibition Era gangster? Does it make you less of a man if you cry when a terrible tragedy hits you? Of course not. Use your common sense—and accept your weaknesses as well as your strengths.

The "Perfect Woman"

American women wrestle with a different kind of obsessive problem. Too many feel they must achieve a kind of physical perfection—or they are unworthy. This is a different side of the same coin, and is equally ridiculous.

As a plastic surgeon, I've met so many beautiful women who thought they were ugly because the slightest blemish was unacceptable to them. Dozens have asked me to operate on deformities that were nonexistent and I've refused to do this, because it would be unethical to take money for doing nothing.

Women do not dread feeling fear or expressing it in their actions. They see nothing wrong in crying now and then. Many are openly nervous and accept it without difficulty. "Weakness" to them is physical imperfection.

In *The Challenge of Being a Woman* (Harper & Row, 1955), Helen Sherman and Marjorie Coe emphasize the social pressures on modern American women: ". . . In a recent issue of a popular women's magazine more than half the pictures of women showed them as decorative only, with not even a suggestion that they ever did any work; only five were women seemingly over forty, while the 20 percent ostensibly working were impractically glamorized."

The authors feel that this goal of physical perfection goes beyond her own self to that of her entire environment. ". . . The typical American home no longer resembles a Currier and Ives lithograph crowded with adults and children having a good time together. It looks instead like a composite advertisement for the latest in furniture, home appliances, wallpaper and broadloom carpeting, with the family seldom all together because one or another of them is elsewhere on achievement bent."

Let's face it: Every woman cannot look like Elizabeth Taylor, and the fact that she doesn't is no cause for inferiority feelings. If she feels she must, she is courting defeat, encouraging the destruction of her self-image.

You women should try to get a fuller perspective of life, developing your spiritual and creative resources, setting goals for your days. Most important, stop blaming yourself if you're not the "perfect woman" that doesn't even exist.

We All Make Mistakes

Any formula for happy living that prescribes 100 percent this-or-that is doomed to failure before it is applied because, as human beings, we cannot measure up to such rigid yardsticks without excess tension. We all make mistakes and we must face up to this realization without bombarding ourselves with self-hatred.

In a Detroit automobile assembly line, perfection is required. One lapse in the mechanics could produce a car that is not safe to drive.

Human beings cannot live up to such perfection and it is not necessary. We are able to function quite well in spite of our shortcomings.

According to the Bible, "My strength is made perfect in weakness."

Please note the phrasing: "made perfect." Nothing about tolerating weakness, but an acknowledgement of the role weakness plays in promoting one's strength.

We all have made mistakes in the past and we will blunder in the future also. We will fall into negative thinking now and then; we will feel hatred and envy when things look black.

If you're a salesman, you'll sometimes use the wrong approach in trying to close a sale.

If you're a mother, you will not always dress the baby properly for the temperature, and she will get a cold.

If you're a student, you'll pass English and history, but do poorly in physics.

If you're an investment counselor, you'll occasionally give a customer unwise counsel.

Mistakes are part of living; you can't always avoid them.

If You Punish Yourself for Your Mistakes, What Do You Gain?

The tragedy is that many people berate themselves for their mistakes—for days, weeks, even for their whole lifetime.

"If I had only not put that money in that property . . ." they say. Or "If I'd only been a little more alert the accident wouldn't have happened . . ."

Re-enacting their failures over and over in their minds, they remind themselves what fools they were, what incompetents. They punish themselves remorselessly in a never-ending castigation that serves no positive purpose.

This self-criticism not only makes them feel miserable, but also afflicts them with nervous tensions that will bring on more mistakes, in a vicious cycle that knows no end.

Some women never stop thinking about a physical imperfection. They dwell on it as if it's the only thing in the world that is real. If their bosom is not the specified size or their nose hooks slightly, their resentment knows no bounds. They punish themselves as if *they* were to blame for this pseudo-calamity.

What do they gain from this? Nothing. What do they lose? The serene power of a healthy self-image.

Stop punishing yourself!

Be Kind to Yourself

Even the most successful men have their limitations.

Former Vice President Richard Nixon played football for unsung Whittier College. He was a tackle but, too light for the position, he was only a second-stringer. He rarely played in a game but, still, he missed few practice sessions and cheered his teammates from the bench for most of four football seasons. Nixon's acceptance of his limitations won the admiration of his football coach and he helped lift the morale of his team.

All men have difficult moments.

Carl Sandburg, the great American poet-author, tells of his

in *Always the Young Strangers:* (Harcourt, Brace & World, Inc., 1952–1953.) "I had my bitter and lonely hours moving out of boy years into a grown young man. I can remember a winter where the thought came often that it might be best to step out of it all. . . .

"After that winter the bitter and lonely hours still kept coming at times, but I had been moving in a slow way to see that to all the best men and women I had known in my life and especially all the great ones that I had read about, life wasn't easy, life had often its bitter and lonely hours, and when you grow with new strength of body and mind it is by struggle."

Life is a bitter struggle indeed, and you can survive happily only if you are kind to yourself. Success is a process of overcoming one's defects and plunging through desertland to an oasis of greenery.

A biographer wrote of Thomas Edison that "Shy or retiring he might be but once he began to talk about an idea or an invention that was close to his heart, he could become surprisingly lucid and even eloquent." (*Edison*, by Matthew Josephson, McGraw Hill Co, 1959.)

A classic case of a man who was kind to his shortcomings and rose through them to great heights is that of our great President, Abraham Lincoln. In *Living Lincoln* (Rutgers University Press, 1955), editors Paul M. Angle and Earl Schenck Miers tell the story of the Lincoln-Douglas debates. "Voters saw two men as different as men could be. Although Douglas was little more than five feet in height his broad shoulders, massive chest and deep musical voice conveyed an impression of strength and sturdiness. Lincoln—thin, bony, awkward—stood a foot above his rival. His voice, as he began to speak, would be high-pitched and nasal but as he warmed to his work the pitch would drop and his words would carry to the outer limits of a crowd of thousands. . . .

"On January 5, 1859 the General Assembly of Illinois confirmed the result of the fall election by returning Stephen A. Douglas to the United States Senate. By this time Lincoln had put defeat behind him and had plunged again into his law practice—partly to make up for the time he had lost and the money he had spent in the preceding six months, and partly to push the memory of failure from his mind. . . .

"But Lincoln could no longer devote himself wholly to law. His debates with Douglas had been reported all over the country. A short six months earlier the name of Abraham Lincoln had hardly been mentioned outside the state of Illinois, now millions knew it. Letters came from strangers asking for Lincoln's views on political questions; others begged for speeches. Despite defeat he had become a man of national prominence."

Here is a wonderful man, whose inner strength shone through his defects—because he accepted his weaknesses and concentrated on the job at hand—because he believed in himself—because he could be kind to himself.

He was a human being, just as you and I: his deification as a political figure was in the future. What he could do, in terms of his concept of himself, you can do—in terms of your own self-evaluation. Maybe you can't be president, but you can be a successful human being.

Accepting Your Weakness
Will Fortify Your Self-Image

If you make peace with your weaknesses, you will fortify your self-image. In ceasing to criticize yourself, you will place emphasis on the "plus" factors in your personality. You will look for things to like in yourself, and you will find them.

These hints will help you:

1. *Learn your limitations.* We all have our breaking points, physical and mental. They vary with the individual; some people can stand up under some forms of pressure, but will buckle under other stresses. Stop criticizing yourself for being "weak" and instead get in the habit of recognizing your limitations.

2. *Honor your limitations.* Once you are aware of your breaking points, use this knowledge to help yourself. Don't push yourself beyond your limits, just to prove to other people that you are courageous! It takes courage to make decisions for yourself, even if some insensitive people may sneer at you.

3. *"Toughness."* Men should not feel that they have to be super-masculine heroes! Most characters of this type are fictional creations, products of writers' lively imaginations. Real-life men have failings as well as strengths. Sometimes troubles will pile up and, in despair, you'll feel like crying. It is nonsense that a man shouldn't cry; liberate yourself from such a foolish belief!

4. *"Perfection."* Women have other attributes more valuable than the physical image one can see in a mirror. Shake free from the superficial thinking that leaves scars on your self-image! You can't afford these scars.

5. *Always be true to yourself.* None of us likes the friend who smiles on us when we're rich and disappears when we've lost our money. It's the same way with yourself. If you admire your own strength and hate your weakness, you're not being true to yourself. Your self-image will never be steady; you'll never be happy. Accept yourself when you hit rock-bottom and you have a foundation for growth.

Look Ahead to a Bright Future

One word of caution here: Do not resign yourself to weakness.

Your strength lies in accepting your weaknesses and then trying to rise above failure to success. When I talk about accepting your weaknesses, I don't mean that you resign yourself to permanent, self-induced inadequacies.

Since most people downgrade themselves and are afraid to go forward, there is a danger that some of you will misunderstand my meaning. I don't admire the Calamity Joes and Calamity Janes in life, always crying in their soup about what terrible things life has done to them.

The purpose of this book is positive, helping you to improve your self-image, so I must clearly point out that in accepting your weaknesses, you accept yourself as a total human being with the assets and liabilities to which you are heir. With full awareness of your limitations, you plan your days optimistically, accepting them and yet rising above them to your full potential strength. You should make peace with your failings, forget about them, and move on to your daily goals—all in the process of living.

Forget the failures of yesterday and the fears of tomorrow —they don't exist! Think of today and achieve something worthwhile—and you'll be strong!

11

How to Be an Individual
in an Age of Conformity

Social critics, in vast numbers, have labeled this "the age of conformity," postulating that modern man, terrified by technological and other forces beyond his control, tries to gain security by imitating the other fellow. He sacrifices his individual identity but achieves a sense of comfort in his feeling of oneness with other human beings.

In *America as a Civilization* (Simon & Schuster, 1957), columnist-educator Max Lerner writes that "Cultural stereotypes are an inherent part of all group living, and they become sharper with mass living. There have always been unthinking people leading formless, atomized lives. What has happened in America is that the economics of mass production has put a premium on uniformity so that America produces more units of more commodities (although sometimes of fewer models) than other cultures. . . .

"The real dangers of the American mode of life are not in the machine or even in standardization as much as they are in conformism. . . ."

Is "rugged individualism" a thing of the past? Are we today puppets which Fate pulls this way and that, controlling our destiny?

The answer to both questions is *no, if* . . . if your self-image allows you the freedom that makes a human being God's proudest creation.

If you enslave yourself to the opinions of others, inhibiting your thoughts and actions, it is because you have no true regard for yourself. Other people must shower approval on you because you do not trust yourself; you must continually act the way you feel others expect you to act because you have no faith in your own standards.

The Pioneer Spirit

Some social scientists approach the subject of "conformity" from a historical standpoint.

They see a relationship between the expansive, optimistic, outgoing American of the nineteenth century and the existence of unclaimed lands in the West which gave the restless spirit somewhere to go.

In those days, they say, a man felt a sense of freedom in living his life. If pressures hemmed him in or if his fellows labeled him a failure, he could always pack up and travel to some less-populated region where he might make a fortune almost overnight.

The pioneers, living in an atmosphere of sudden death and sudden wealth, were individualists.

Theodore Roosevelt wrote about the early ranchmen, "Yet there was not only much that was attractive in their wild, free, reckless lives but there was also very much good about the men themselves. They were frank, bold and self-reliant to a degree. They feared neither man, brute, nor element."

The wild life had negative aspects, too: when unrestrained self-interest flared up and people flouted civilized codes, violence snuffed out lives swiftly.

Still, the pioneers were cheerful people who lived dynamic, though numbered, days. If the newly evolving society's rules were too strict, the open spaces of unsettled lands offered them refuge.

Lerner believed that "Self-reliance, courage, alertness, obstinate endurance, friendliness, a democratic informality are traits that emerged from the continuous cycles of land settlement."

"Home on the Range," once reputedly President Franklin Delano Roosevelt's favorite song, admirably captured this spirit.

End of the Frontier

With the end of the nineteenth century the frontier, geographically speaking, came to an end, but many areas were sparsely populated. During this century people have emigrated to these pockets of opportunity, filling them up. Texas, which in 1900 had a population of slightly less than three million, in 1960 boasted over nine million. California, whose population was about one and a half million in 1900, reported a 1960 population of over fifteen and a half million. More and more, the open spaces have been occupied and dissatisfied people have not had a land of opportunity as barren as they used to have.

Railroads have long since joined together big cities and out-of-the-way spots. Airplanes have further narrowed the gap, timewise, and radio and television have invaded small-town outposts with big city values.

If civilized pressures plague you today, there is no longer an easy way out—at least not in this heavily populated country. But do not let this cause you the slightest despair. *This need not be the end of your frontier; you need not pull in your horizons.* Inside you, you have powers that dwarf any of the phenomena just described. Perhaps they have been lying dormant within you, waiting for proper cultivation.

This is important to remember when you feel depressed: *Thinking, mental picturing, about yourself and about your world, here is your great secret weapon.* Read this chapter thoroughly and you will begin stockpiling ammunition that will fortify you to be your own person in this mechanical age.

If this is what you want, you can do it.

"Keeping Up with the Joneses"

Actually, living in modern society is simple if we know how. In certain areas, we must conform to the rules of the group. There is no alternative, if we are to be accepted as worthy members of our civilization. At the same time, there are other areas in which we are free to express the basic individuality which separates us from others.

One of the great errors in modern life is people's over-estimation and overapplication of the first area; too many people buy the latest model car because their neighbors did or move into a certain style house for the same reason, a phenomenon popularly known as "keeping up with the Joneses."

There's an illuminating passage in Vance Packard's big-seller, *The Status Seekers* (David McKay Co., 1959): "While observing the 1958 convention of the nation's home builders in Chicago, I heard one of the featured speakers, a home-marketing consultant, report that he and his aides had conducted 411 'depth interviews' in eight cities to find what people are seeking when they buy a home. In many cases, he reported, mid-century home buyers are buying themselves a symbol of success, and he discussed at length strategies for giving a house being offered for sale 'snob appeal.'

"Many other experts in home selling have recently cited 'snob appeal' as one of the great secret weapons. One strategy, he said, is to drop some French phrases in your advertisement. French, he explained, is the language of the snob. Later in the year, we began seeing newspaper advertisement of housing developers drenched in French."

If you over-conform like this, you cannot be happy, because you are not living your own life at all. *You are living someone else's and thus you're only partly yourself.*

Conformity, however, need not be a negative word; it can be a positive one. Civilizations endure because there is a certain amount of positive conformity from its citizenry.

"We are members one of another," we find in the Bible.

By conformity, in its helpful sense, I don't mean being like someone else, but agreeing to share with others the wonders of the world—if we agree that there are limits to this process.

This is fruitful conformity, a vitamin pill that gives us all sustenance.

Conformity, in the true sense, means helping each other without stepping on each other's toes—or stepping on your own toes. It is an active concept, rooted in the life-giving feeling of liking your neighbor and experiencing compassion for others. It is a token of brotherly love, in which one gives of himself instead of sitting around waiting for someone to give to him.

We Must Conform to Certain Rules

Living among people and compartmentalized in living space, we must follow certain rules which are for the common good. We must honor others' property and drive an automobile safely; we must not set fire to our neighbors' house if we are angry at them.

On the job, a man must often watch his step. If your boss is an envious man and he drives a five-year-old Ford, it might be dangerous for you to show up for work driving a brand-new Cadillac. By the same line of reasoning, at your office Christmas party, your wife might cost you your job if she comes in a gorgeous $85 dress when your boss' wife is dressed more simply.

"Making a living" means just that: the man of the family, the "breadwinner," is earning the money that insures his family's very existence and in this area a person must sometimes be very cautious. If you work for a large corporation, conforming to certain rules may be essential if you are not to lose your job.

Working women also may encounter similar pressures, as may mothers engaged in community activities.

Many of you, however, have huge areas of freedom which you do nothing to exploit. You give about eight hours a day to your job, but that leaves you eight in which to relax and eight in which you can sleep. There is nothing in the contract that says you have to sleep on the same kind of pillow the boss uses, or smoke the same kind of cigars he likes. There is nothing in the contract that says you can't buy an air conditioner because his wife hates air conditioning. Your conforming ends when you leave your job to go home and you can balance this conforming by developing your individual thoughts and resources when you are away from the job.

You can plan the future for your wife and children—your way. You can relate to your friends—your way. You can think your own thoughts and work on your own hobbies and, in your own home you are a king and your wife is the queen.

In your community, your active conformity in projects that *you* believe in, the spirit of brotherly love that you give to such enterprises is the positive type of conformity I mentioned earlier, one that can develop your personality in healthful channels if you have the courage of your convictions. In these activities, too, you can express your uniqueness as you participate in group causes.

You Can Be Yourself

So, actually, you do have wide areas in which to express your own unique personality and to be yourself. Too many adults fail to take advantage of these opportunities for growth, preferring instead to submerge themselves in the herd.

Allen Funt, the originator of "Candid Camera," said recently (*TV Guide*, "Allen Funt's Candid Kids," June 22, 1963), "Children are beautiful. . . . They're so original, so independent. They're *everything* you wish adults were. But adults are consistently herd-minded, conformant, subject to group pressure. They're moving in the wrong direction. They're moving away from individualism toward the herd." Funt contrasts two film clips for "Candid Camera." One shows a man walking up a "down" escalator. Another adult shortly follows him until, unquestioningly, a group of adults tramps up the "down" escalator.

The second film clip illustrates the greater individuality of children. "A child walks up to a large, empty box. He inspects it carefully, decides it's a fortress. He gets into it and shoots away at the enemy. Another child strolls up to the box. He decides it's a house, gets into it and plays grownup. A third child sees the box, decides it's a roller coaster, and gleefully slides it down an incline. . . ."

Why not recapture your individuality, which is your birthright? After you have fulfilled your responsibilities to your community, how about treating yourself as fairly and exploring your avenues of personal self-development?

A few years ago I spent a day at the seashore. It was a sunny day, with blue skies, and I was enjoying the beach, talking to friends, watching people leaping the waves. Nearby a young married couple with a young baby were putting down a blanket. The mother put the baby down and off the little one went, staggering on her uncertain little baby legs.

Her face dead serious, she wobbled up to a family sitting in deck chairs and, to my surprise, picked up a child's chair and carried it over to her amused parents. She then turned around and, with startling accuracy, carried it back to where she'd picked it up. She then climbed up on it (with difficulty), sat down regally and, with serious calm, surveyed the world.

I found myself laughing delightedly at her spontaneous, individual purposefulness. She was herself, so unlike adults who spend their lives trying to do what they think people expect of them.

As adults, we must respect personal property more than does this baby, but we also can learn from her a lesson in the art of cultivating *our own personalities,* which should spring fresh from our inner being.

You Owe It to Yourself to Be an Individual

Deep down, no two people are exactly alike, and you owe it to yourself to develop your individuality. There are too many "carbon-copy" people these days; be an original!

This does not mean you should be an eccentric. I certainly do not mean that you must grow a beard or get up on a soapbox and deliver lectures.

Dwight Eisenhower is very much himself and people love him for it. He is a simple man, above pretentiousness. As a military leader, his humility was remarkable.

In *My Friend Ike* (Frederick Fell Inc, 1956), his Army subordinate Marty Snyder tells of Eisenhower's visit to his restaurant after World War II:

"When General Eisenhower returned from Europe, he came to the restaurant for dinner. As we sat together, I told him how much I wanted to see him become president, and I admitted that I was talking to a lot of people about it.

"He laughed. He said, 'Look, Marty, I'm a soldier and that's all I want to be.' 'General,' I said, 'I never wanted to be a soldier, but they drafted me. I guess you can be drafted

145

to run for President, if it comes to that.' 'I'm sure it won't,' he said."

Ike was just being himself.

Have a Mind of Your Own!

Your mind is one of your most precious possessions; don't give it up by default! Think your own thoughts, not what you believe others want you to think.

According to John Stuart Mill, renowned nineteenth century English essayist-philosopher, "If all mankind minus one, were of one opinion and only one person were of the contrary opinion, mankind would be no more justified in silencing that one person than he, if he had the power, would be justified in silencing mankind."

Your inner thoughts especially are yours to own. Living in civilized society, there are sometimes restraints on your actions, but never on your inner thoughts.

"My mind to me a kingdom is," wrote Sir Edward Dyer, sixteenth century English poet.

Make your mind a kingdom, not a jail! Let your thoughts be free as birds that fly in the sky; don't censure them and criticize them and hate yourself if they don't always fall in with the pocket of majority opinion, as you know it.

Learn to Keep Your Identity in a Crowd

Some people have the inner strength to feel their own individuality when alone, but give up their identity in a crowd of people.

Is this you? When you express an opinion at a social gathering and someone else laughs at it, do you keep silent and slink off into a shell? If you do, digest these ideas as if they were a good meal. They will give you a different kind of energy, the power to keep your individual identity in a crowd of people.

1. *Recognize your right to differ.* This is a democracy and we all have this right, but many people do not exercise it.

Stop playing follow the leader! When you disagree with the majority, some people may criticize you but a mature person will not inhibit himself when others frown, or sell himself for a few approving smiles.

2. *Give yourself approval.* You've got to be your best friend. You can't always count on the other person, even if he's a good fellow, because he's got his own interests to look after and inner problems may be eating at him. Only you can fully give yourself the acceptance you need and fortify yourself with the "heart" one must have to maintain identity in a crowd.

3. *Don't fear the bully!* Almost all people are decent, if you give them a fair chance. Still, fearful people sometimes discover unscrupulous tactics that win them status. Some exploit the tendency of people to feel inferior, dominating crowds of people with verbal brilliance, and a threat of ridiculing potential competitors. Learn to withstand verbal taunts and stand up for your right to express your beliefs and your feelings. Remember that deep down the bully is afraid, and his attacks are defensive cover-ups.

4. *Visualize your successes!* Some days you won't be feeling so good or you just won't get along so well with a specific crowd of people. You might feel like an outsider. Don't be depressed! This happens to everybody once in a while. You can restore your confidence if you'll picture happier moments, when you felt freer and more alive. If the mind pictures won't come at first, keep trying. It's worth the effort.

People Who Stuck to Their Guns—and Won

Life has no rose-strewn lanes leading to a door marked SUCCESS. It's more an up-and-down struggle with grayish graduations of accomplishments.

Former heavyweight champion Joe Louis knew days of bleak poverty as a child in the South.

The great politician Al Smith fought his way out of the slums to power and honor.

Satchell Paige, the remarkable Negro pitcher, had his greatness obscured for many years when baseball was still a segregated affair.

The very talented Jackie Gleason knew poverty as a child and another bright TV star, Dick Van Dyke, once knew near-penniless days.

Others have fought their way up to successful positions in life, and maintained their individuality in the process.

A man courageous enough to stand alone is the hero of the movie "High Noon." The small-town sheriff, deserted by his friends, has to stand alone against the band of killers returning to town. Scared, he conquers his fears and subdues the outlaws. This case is fictional—but true to life nevertheless.

Has ever a man sustained himself better in the face of criticism than Harry Truman? I doubt it. He refused to be typed, stuck to his convictions and ignored the attacks of his critics. Newspapers insulted his ability and even politicians doubted him, but *he kept faith in himself.*

In *The Man From Missouri* (G. P. Putnam's Sons, 1962), Alfred Steinberg reports on a meeting between Truman and Winston Churchill:

(Churchill): "The last time you and I sat across the conference table was at Potsdam, Mr. President."

Truman nodded agreement.

Churchill's tone changed.

"I must confess, sir, I held you in very low regard then. I loathed your taking the place of Franklin Roosevelt."

Truman's wide grin vanished.

"I misjudged you badly."

Churchill went on after a long pause:

"Since that time you, more than any other man, have saved western civilization."

Churchill's initial estimate of Truman was the popular one. According to Steinberg, "No matter how momentous his actions or how unswerving his dedication to basic principles many politicians failed to take Truman seriously. Some could not accept the fact that he was President. . . .

"And when the nation was stunned by Franklin Roosevelt's death on April 12, 1945, part of this emotional shock was attributed to the realization of who had succeeded him. Yet within Harry Truman's lifetime, historians agree that he must be ranked with the strongest of American Presidents."

Truman's "rugged individualism" never passed a stiffer test than in his Presidential victory over Thomas Dewey. Counted out by pollsters and the nation's press, he kept insisting that he would win the country's mandate. He trailed Dewey in early returns and newspaper headlines even announced a Dewey win, but Truman calmly went to sleep and was not even surprised when he woke up to find he had won.

Over-conforming Distorts Your Self-Image

In the Bible, we find the assertions that "We are members one of another" and "if a House be divided against itself, that house cannot stand."

These sage comments tell us why a basic measure of conformity is prerequisite for the continuance of civilized life as we know it.

Over-conforming, too much a part of modern life, is something entirely different. It is a sacrifice of individual identity when this surrender accomplishes no worthwhile purpose.

When you over-conform, you distort your self-image. You no longer really know who you are at all, because you are always trying to please others. Looking for constant approval when you don't need it, bowing and scraping to relieve your anxiety, you twist out of shape the unique qualities that make you an individual.

To be happy, you must have areas in which you can express your uniqueness without fear of realistic danger. These areas exist, if you don't take them away from yourself. When you find them, you will be finding a part of yourself that will make you feel more whole. Your self-image will be on more solid ground, and you will be happier.

12

How to Function Successfully Under Pressure

It is likely that the world has never seen such days of pressure. The possibility of mass destruction is always with us; we must learn to live with the realistic dangers of the twentieth century.

The Balkans used to be known as the "powder keg of Europe" and an incident in this area set off the explosion that ignited World War I.

Today the whole world is a "powder keg" and one awesome explosion could kill millions of people in minutes.

The specter of the atomic and hydrogen bombs hangs over us; each day brings new diplomatic crises which affect us. In addition to these technological terrors, this is an era of turmoil, with changes in morality, breakdown of the family and movements of social unrest, as downtrodden peoples increasingly assert their rights all over the world.

A noted nuclear physicist recently stated that we are today in a period of extremely rapid change, technological and social, one almost unprecedented in the annals of history.

The September 24, 1963 issue of *Look Magazine* featured an article outlining today's stresses. "Each of us must make difficult moral decisions. We are witnessing the death of the old morality. In our world of masses of people, jet-age travel, nuclear power and fragmented families, conditions are changing so fast that the established, moral guidelines have been yanked from our hands." ("Morality, U.S.A.," by J. Robert Moskin.)

Some contemporary developments have positive possibilities, too. Nuclear energy can be used constructively, as a source of power bringing increasing comfort to people. The fight to end racial and color discrimination is a noble one, when executed without violence, and the August 28, 1963, civil rights demonstration in Washington was a dignified, forward-looking action. The terrifying weapons we have today can be optimistically regarded as deterrents to future world wars because such holocausts would be unthinkable.

Still, the pressures do exist. To deny this would be to stick one's head in the sand, ostrich-like, in defense against fear.

Life Is a Series of Crises

Aside from global problems, life is a series of minor and major crises.

If you're a mother with young children, one moment you may be relaxing with a healthy family, only to find that an hour later the baby may have an alarming temperature of 104 degrees.

If you're the family breadwinner, a secure job with a prosperous corporation may be suddenly endangered when it agrees to merge with another concern, with job cuts in the offing to reduce operating expenses.

If you're retired, living on a small pension, your purchasing power may dwindle as the cost of living rises. Having a fixed income, you may worry about money almost constantly.

No matter who you are, each week usually brings problems. To live happily, you must accept them as part of reality and bend your energies to cope with them. You cannot shut them out or refuse to see them—if you do, you are pulling away from life into a living death. You cannot expect to solve them permanently and "live happily ever after." This is childishly omnipotent thinking, a carryover of baby-carriage days.

You must face up to life. Each day you must get up out of bed, recharge your batteries with a nourishing breakfast, and set out on a day full of pitfalls as well as promises, pain as well as plenty.

You must plan your daily goals with fresh courage, and keep on plugging until you attain their maximum realization.

What Is Your Pressure-Toleration Quotient?

A basic question here is: How much pressure can you tolerate? What is your own, individual breaking point?

This is a subtle question and there is no absolute answer to it. One's ability to function is not as measurable as time. It varies with inner conditions, physical and mental.

One thing is certain, however. Many people do break down under the stresses of modern life. Our crowded mental institutions bear witness to this statement. Many other people stagger along, functioning marginally, feeling vaguely upset about what is going on around them and inside them, addicted to poor habits of eating, drinking, smoking, and relying too much on medicines.

How about the successful people? How do they handle stressful situations?

Simply put, they are able to rise above crises by relaxing no matter what the external situation. Their belief in themselves, the strength of their self-image is impenetrable armor which protects them against shattering events.

The Secret of Winning

This is their big secret: the ability to remain calm when others feel harassed and confused. They are able to feel secure regardless of pressures; their self-image holds up.

In *Your Thoughts Can Change Your Life* (Prentice-Hall, 1961), Donald Curtis writes about Bing Crosby's calm in an emergency:

"Many years ago, when I was beginning as a radio actor in Hollywood, I was called for a small part on a show on which Bing Crosby was the guest star. He was his usual relaxed self right up to air time. The rest of us, however, all felt the mounting tension as we waited for the producer to give the signal that we were on the air.

"The producer raised his arm for the signal. Then with only

ten seconds to go, Bing dropped the script. Panic broke loose —in everyone but Bing. While actors, agency men, stage hands and musicians scrambled to pick up the fluttering pages of the script, Bing nonchalantly bent down, picked up the elusive first page, cocked his hat on the back of his head, and came in exactly on cue. That night he gave a tremendous performance without any fuss whatsoever."

You must also be able to adapt yourself to changing conditions. Sometimes, to succeed, you must change your plans.

In *The Road to Successful Living,* Louis Binstock tells an amusing story about the famous American artist James McNeill Whistler:

> In 1854 he was a cadet at West Point on his way to a career of soldiering. In Chemistry class one afternoon he was asked to discuss silicon. He rose and began, "Silicon is a gas."
>
> "That will do, Mr. Whistler," said his instructor.
>
> A few weeks later Cadet Whistler was dicharged from the Academy.
>
> Years later, when he was quite famous as a painter, he liked to say, "If silicon had been a gas, I would have been a general."

The Story of My First Patient

During my sixty-odd years of living, I've had my share of crises. One was the turning point of my life.

When I came back from my postgraduate studies in Berlin, Vienna, Paris, Rome and London, I opened up an office on lower Fifth Avenue in New York City. At the time very few people—even physicians—knew about plastic surgery, so I was taking a chance entering this embryo profession. I furnished five large rooms as best I could with my limited funds. I then put up a shingle outside my door and waited for my first patient.

I had operated successfully on many patients in Europe during my training and, despite the newness of my field, I figured that I would be an overnight success. I thought that my services would be in immediate demand.

I waited. There were no telephone calls during the morning —none at all. As the afternoon wore on I ate a leisurely lunch but felt impatient. I began staring at the telephone, hoping to mobilize it into action, but I couldn't force it to ring. Then, toward the end of the day, the phone rang and I dived for it.

"How are you doing?" It was my mother.

"Okay," I said, my spirits falling.

During my first week, there was not a single phone call, except toward the end of the day when my mother called to ask how I was making out. As much as I liked my mother, her voice became more and more an omen of doom.

This went on for three weeks. My office was a quiet as a morgue and my telephone seemed an unnecessary extravagance, an object that I resented. Slowly, my confidence in myself began to fade and I felt nervous and worried. For the first time in my life, I knew panic.

What was my fear? To make ends meet, I'd have to make at least $500 the first month, including a small check I wanted to send my mother to show her how successful I was. I had no cash reserve to tide me over more than this one-month period.

As the fourth week began, I became obsessed with the fear that I would be a failure, that all my years of training would prove a waste of time, energy and money. In another week, I would have to close my office unless I got a patient. In my mind's eye, I visualized the taunts and reprimands of my mother, my relatives, and my friends, all of whom had advised me to become a general practitioner or to train in a better-known specialty, where the future would be more sure.

It was my first great crisis. I didn't know what to do. Slumping in my chair, I looked out the window. Across the street a new building was going up and I watched a laborer going up to the fourth or fifth floor on an elevator, carrying bricks. His job looked dangerous and in those pre-union days his salary probably was slim, but for a moment I wished I could junk all my medical training and change places with him, just so that I could feel the security of an assured wage. Grimly, I sat and waited and waited.

Shrilly, the phone rang out. As I picked it up, I glumly said to myself, "It's mother!"

But it wasn't. It was a doctor, a childhood friend. He had heard of my work from my family and he had a patient for me. He asked when he could bring him over.

Although I felt desperately dependent on this case, I summoned up my courage and adopted a professional manner. "Just a moment!" I said. "Let me look at my appointment book!"

I looked at the empty pages for thirty seconds, then said, "I have time for you right now. Come right over!"

Shaving quickly, I put on a white coat and waited for my first patient. I forced myself to be calm, forgetting my urgent need and remembering my surgical skill, seeing what I could do for a patient.

I thought he'd never come and was beginning to fidget in my armchair when the doorbell finally rang. There was the doctor and a young man with a severely bashed-in nose, a lifelong reminder of a childhood accident. He was a shoe salesman, in his twenties, and he felt depressed about his appearance and concerned about the difficulty he had breathing properly.

My panic was entirely gone. All I felt was a professional interest in helping the man. I looked at his nose in my examining chair, saw quickly that I could perform a successful operation and then we agreed on a fee.

My crisis was over. Somehow I had lived through the toughest month in my life and survived my anxiety. My second case was not long coming and soon I was an established plastic surgeon.

How I Helped an Actress Overcome Stage Fright

A few years ago I was in California, ready to fly to Europe over the North Pole.

I went backstage to see the star of a musical comedy about to open in Los Angeles, a well-known actress. She was feeling the pressure of opening night. She was panicky, felt she couldn't perform, was certain she would lose her voice. She told me she could barely move her feet she felt so paralyzed.

"What's wrong?" I asked.

"I suddenly get this panicky feeling. I usually get nervous before going on, but this is different."

"What's so different?"

"Doctor, I don't know. I'm afraid I'm losing my voice."

"Do you know your lines?"

"Of course."

"Do you know your songs?"

"Yes."

"Then what's the matter?"

"I don't know. A fear came over me that I won't reach my high notes in the songs."

We were in her dressing room, filled with beautiful costumes, a huge dressing table and mirror at the side, flowers in vases from admirers. A maid flitted back and forth arranging her costume changes.

She looked at herself in the mirror, began singing and stopped.

"Go on," I said.

"I can't, I just can't." She began to cry.

What could I do to help her? I wondered. I had no drugs to calm her, and there was no time to send out for anything.

"Well, don't worry," I said. "You're a real pro and you'll get over your attack of nerves. I have just the right thing for you in my bag. It's a new drug and will work quickly."

Telling myself that this white lie was necessary, I took a sterilized syringe from my black bag, broke a small glass vial of distilled water and sucked it up into the syringe.

I gave the actress an injection and promised her it would take immediate effect. "Sit down," I said, "and relax."

When a stage assistant poked his head in a few minutes later to prepare her to go onstage, she was calm.

"What wonderful medicine this is! I could kiss you for it!" She did. "I feel wonderful, doctor, and I'm so grateful!"

She went on stage and gave a marvelous performance.

Later, at a dinner party to celebrate the opening, I went over to her table. "Do you know, that was one of your best performances!"

"Thanks to you," she said.

"No, thanks to you. You did it, not me. Do you know that the medicine I gave you was only distilled water?"

She turned pale, then she laughed. Ever since she has felt nervous at times, but never hysterical, for she would remember that night when, with only imaginary help, she pulled herself out of a crisis and won the applause of the audience and critics.

Today she is still one of the big talents in show business.

Set Your Goals

To function successfully under trying conditions, you must concentrate on realizable goals for which you have enthusiasm. These serve as propellants to keep you going when things get tough and eliminate conflicting thoughts which destroy your calm.

In a football game, for example, suppose a team has the ball on its opponents' three-yard line, first down and goal to go. Three times they try to score, but the other team is muscular and determined and they don't gain a foot. The offensive team needs a touchdown to win the game; a field goal won't do. In the face of such fierce resistance in this pressure situation, they could feel like giving up. If they didn't really care, they would. It is only the intensity with which they seek their goal, a touchdown, that gives them a chance to realize it. With this goal set firmly in eleven minds, they will figure every possible avenue to getting across the goal line. Even if they don't succeed, they will have the satisfaction of knowing they did their best.

Life is like football: you must set your goals. You must set in motion your success mechanism.

When I was sweating it out, waiting for my first patient, this one factor helped me: *I knew what I wanted.*

The actress, paralyzed with fright on opening night, shared this spur to successful functioning. Since her objective was clear, she needed just a little support to get her over the top.

In *10 Days to a Great New Life* (Prentice-Hall, 1963), William Edwards emphasizes the importance of goal setting: He relates: "One of the most enterprising companies in America—the leader in its field—requires all 50 of its vice-presidents to write down their specific goals—short-range, medium-range, and long-range. It keeps things stirred up, gets everyone thinking ahead. It spurs the imagination to picture an effective future. It plants the 'image seed' of things to come. It's made the company explosively successful."

Once you know what you want, you have reached first base and you feel the security that goes with this accomplishment. The next question is, how intense is your desire to achieve these goals?

Believe in Your Goals

The firmer your belief in your goals, the better you will do. When your determination is sharply channelized, you can move aggressively and act with calmness at the same time.

General Douglas MacArthur had this belief. "From the day of his confident parting message to the Filipinos, (I shall return) no deviation from MacArthur's singleminded plan is discernible. Every battle action in New Guinea, every air raid on Rabaul or PT-boat attack on Japanese barges in the Bismarck Sea were a mere preliminary for the reconquest of the Philippines." (MacArthur 1941–1951, by Charles A. Willoughby and John Chamberlain, McGraw Hill, 1954.)

You may never be a general—or even a PFC. (God willing!)—but you can believe just as fervently in your aims, and they are no less noble. An automobile mechanic who cares when a stranger brings in a malfunctioning car and who tries to do a clean, complete job is a good man. His belief in what he's doing will help him keep calm and weather crises.

Bring Back Your Triumphs

You've read this earlier in this book, but I can't emphasize it often enough: You'll help yourself if you'll bring back into your mind your better moments, picturing the details of situations that were happy and successful for you. Focusing on these images will bring you peace during tense times; it will aid in the building up of your self-image.

While I was waiting for my first patient and it seemed that no one knew my phone number, I had to battle to keep my confidence in myself. My best weapon was an image of myself operating flawlessly during my training days, and I saturated my mind with this mental picture until I reached my objective.

I can't say what was in the actress' mind but, once I had given her support, I'm sure that her recollection of previous moments of stardom helped her go on stage and give a great performance.

You might be thinking, "But I've never been a dramatic success—nothing like that at all."

Yes, but you're not going to perform on the stage in front of thousands of people. You are going to perform just on the stage of your mind—again and again—until you are able to bring your most successful picture into reality.

You don't have to be an actress or a doctor. You have to be only yourself, operating realistically in your own potential areas of competence, withdrawing wealth from your bank of experience, the bank that pays off with interest.

Don't Be Afraid to Be Nervous!

Sometimes you'll be nervous, no matter who you are. What do you do then? You simply accept it and keep going until you regain your self-assurance.

Nervousness is not a terrible thing at all—unless you think it is. When you feel nervous, remember that you're not alone in this respect.

According to Dr. Peter P. Steincrohn (*How to Master Your Fears,* Wilfred Funk, 1952), "The world is sick with fear. The best way to combat fear is to recognize it—and then face up to it. The first step is for us—each and every one of us (morons excepted)—to admit that we are frightened. That in itself will bring some measure of relief."

Comedian Paul Lynde has even made a career out of nervousness. *TV Guide* reports: "Certainly he is the only performer ever to pay a press agent good money to write of him: 'Paul [was known] as one of the worst nervous shambles in show business, both while performing and in private life. Even now, after two years of psychotherapy, he says, "if I ever completely lost my nervousness I would be frightened half to death." ' " ("Paul Lynde's Traumatic Success," July 13, 1963.)

I'm not telling you that if you get the shakes Perry Como will hire you for his TV show, as he did Paul Lynde, and I'm certainly not advising you to induce nervousness in yourself. But if your nerves should be on edge and you can't help showing it, so what? That's my main point; don't blame yourself!

Your Power in a Crisis

Once you have set goals that you believe in, brought into your mind success pictures of the past, and prepared yourself to accept your human weaknesses, you will feel power in a crisis. You will feel capable of dealing with situations as they arise.

You have powers inside you that will help you deal with emergencies. Once you are wholehearted in your determination to succeed, and once you have pinpointed your goals, you are in a position to mobilize these powers.

Your success mechanism is now ready to help you carry the ball. Having given it clearly defined objectives, basically in the form of mental pictures, you have set in motion this automatic servo-mechanism. It will work for your welfare—and difficult situations will not destroy the efficiency of this marvelous power which resides within all of you.

You need not let crises floor you; you can overcome your fears and deal realistically with your world.

Practice Exercise No. 6: Living with Crises

This exercise will help you pull through many a crisis, with steadily decreasing anxiety, if you work at it.

You know the procedure by now; you're in as quiet a place as you can find and you're as relaxed as you can make yourself.

Once more, enter the playhouse of your mind and rummage around in your backlog of motion pictures, real-life films made from the events of your life. Dig out a "horror" story, a Frankenstein story in terms of your alarm, and examine it! It's a crisis scene, one of the many little crises in your life, but you over-reacted out of all proportion to the reality, inflating irritation into a Frankenstein monster of terror.

Perhaps your husband has said he'd be home before midnight and you were still waiting up at two in the morning, your imagination full of dread fantasies.

Or maybe you'd argued with your wife over coffee and, just before you left for the office, she shouted that she was going home to her mother and that she never wanted to see you again. You drove to work, your mind full of dire possibilities, though you knew she just had a bad temper.

Or your boss had looked at you searchingly one time after you had made a mistake and set a severe deadline for your next assignment. Your mind became obsessed with the fear that he was preparing to fire you.

Bring the mental picture of this minor crisis back into your mind and feel your terror. *Feel* it. Recall your morbid thoughts, and fear now as you did then. Remember the frightening possibilities that took over your mind as you conjured up all the nasty things that could happen to you. React to your mental pictures as you did then, with such deep feeling that your physical symptoms of that period return; the palpitating of your heart, the sudden flow of perspiration, turning pale, nausea, whatever your symptoms were—if there were any.

It is not pleasant to re-experience your over-reaction to this small crisis, but it will help you.

Why? Because nine times out of ten one's fears—even in a problem moment—are not remotely justified. Your negative mental imaging was your worst enemy.

Now, bring back what really happened. Feel once again your relief that the worst had not happened, that your imagination had been your enemy. *Feel* it. Relax, as in waking up from a bad dream, realizing it wasn't real, that you're safe. Understand that this life-or-death feeling had little basis in reality, that we all face problems and crises, that your negative imaging is the chief culprit.

Practice along these lines over and over and you'll produce inner changes in yourself that will amaze you. Picture a different situation each day, feel the over-reactive panic, then the relief when reality discloses the negative workings of your imagination.

The more you work on this exercise, the more you will understand that the real crisis is in your mind, part of your inadequate self-image. When you meet situations that currently unnerve you, question the validity of your anxious response and picture events in the past to which you over-reacted. This will help you put the present in better focus, calming you and increasing your ability to function effectively.

As you mature, replacing negative picturing with successful imaging, setting worthwhile goals for yourself, and strengthening your self-image, you will handle difficult situations more competently.

Call on these two old friends to help you pull through major and minor crises.

1. *Truth.* The truth is that we are rarely involved in "life-or-death" emergencies; realizing this may keep you calm when you would otherwise be undermining your positive side with anxiety.

2. *Imagination.* Man is blessed with this faculty, but so often uses it negatively. Be a king in your own mind and you'll be all right.

13

Winning Friends
Can Be Easy for You

About four centuries ago, the great English scholar Francis Bacon, writing about friendship, commented that "It redoubleth joys and cutteth griefs in halfs."

Hundreds of years later, English poet S. T. Coleridge wrote that "Friendship is a sheltering tree."

Friendship is just as important today—maybe it's even more vital because of the strain under which we live. I'm not talking about "fair weather" comradeship, but about the loyal, "through-thick-and-thin" mutual supportiveness that is the meat of good human relatedness.

The man who has sincere friendships is richer than the millionaire or the billionaire—no amount of money can alter this. This may sound like a cliché, but it is an unquestionable truth. You can lose your money. Of course you can lose good friends too—they can die—but if you have the capacity for friendship, you can always make new ones. Moreover, you can lose a good friend only physically; if you loved him, he will remain always in your heart.

Will Rogers is supposed to have once remarked, "I've never met a man I didn't like."

This sentimental statement comes from a man whose simple, generous nature won him the love of a nation. It touches one's heart—because it is friendly.

Life Is People

Life is more than a heartbeat, or the ability to breathe, eat, see and feel. An individual's life rotates around the quality of his relationships with other people. Life is people, and it is not so much what they do for you as what you do for them and what you give each other.

Psychologists, in assessing the traits that make for a well-adjusted human being, place high value on his ability to reach out and relate to other people. The person who can't get along with others is at a grave disadvantage vocationally; many avenues are closed to him. Living in a prison of his own making, he walls off his feelings and cremates his resources. His soul cannot soar: when his moods change, he moves from Alcatraz to Sing Sing.

He cannot live with people, yet he is unable to live happily without them. If he shuts himself off in an "ivory tower," he feels a sense of deprivation that he cannot long deny. If he mingles with the crowd, he feels inhibited and his relationships lack satisfaction. Some people feel the loneliest when people surround them. This is understandable; a person feels more contact in the company of one trusted friend with whom he can be himself than at a large gathering where he feels he must wear a mask.

An individual who is capable of building *real* friendships is a happy man. Even if he doesn't make much money, he is content, reaping the rewards of sweet human relationships. The word "friendship" is one of the warmest words in the English language.

The Art of Winning Friends

Books on the art of friendship crowd our library shelves. They contain suggestions that are fairly helpful, concepts that could induce you to become a more accepting, considerate person.

In the best-selling *How to Win Friends and Influence People*, (Simon & Schuster 1936) Dale Carnegie quotes, with approval, a statement of Henry Ford's. "If there is any one secret of success, it lies in the ability to get the other person's point of view and see things from his angle as well as your own."

Carnegie himself states: *"You can make more friends in two months by becoming interested in other people than you can in two years by trying to get other people interested in you."*

In *Personality and Successful Living*, (Bruce Publishing Co. 1945) James A. Magner's approach is similar. "We come to tolerate, to understand and to love people not by waiting for them to serve us, much less by giving them an opportunity to display their defects, but by assuming the active role ourselves and giving others positive reasons for tolerating and loving us. Nothing wins friends so much as an unselfish concern on our part. Nothing makes us so worthy of friendship as developing ourselves, our resources, our personality by a program of friendliness and usefulness to others."

These are positive ideas. The writers know people and their suggestions are worthwhile.

But, basically, your ability to form sincere, enduring friendships depends on the strength of your self-image.

If You Like Yourself, Others Will

You can learn to be more considerate; this is a fine quality.

You can go out of your way to be useful to other people; this will help.

There are other constructive moves you can make to win friendships. You can master a variety of social skills; you can volunteer to share your material possessions.

But the core of your capacity for friendship is in your thinking about yourself. If you like yourself, others will usually share your feeling. If you despise yourself, so will other people.

By liking yourself, I don't mean the narcissistic form of infantile self-admiration, in which the individual's love centers on himself, to the exclusion of others. You can't *really* like yourself unless you like others.

If you short-change yourself, however, chances are you'll do the same thing to other people.

"Without confidence there is no friendship," wrote the ancient Greek philosopher Epicurus.

True, and confidence has its beginning in one's attitude toward himself!

Why Be Shy?

The shy person finds it difficult to make friends, generally. Inhibiting his free expression, out of fear, he limits his contacts with other people.

Martin Tolchin's description is poignant in "The Roots of Shyness." (*New York Times* Magazine, June 19, 1960.)

"He is a quiet child—too quiet, and too well-behaved. He lacks the 'bellyful of fire' that the late William Bryon Mowery thought all small boys had—or should have. Instead he stands wistfully on the sidelines, unable to wade into the rough and tumble savored by a boy among boys.

"Left to his own devices he may outgrow his shyness, or learn to live with it. Or he may abandon effort to establish contact with the rest of the world.

"The experience can be humbling. Shyness can come between a man and the woman he needs. It can undermine his usefulness to society by preventing him from getting the job for which he qualifies. It can place an intelligent, accomplished person in the position of a social beggar who is thrown conversational crumbs at functions he cannot evade."

Unfortunately, there are many shy people in this world. Life can teach, but it can also frighten people, driving them into shells.

If you are shy, you can learn to be more outgoing. It is, once again, mainly a question of changing your false truth about yourself—because shyness is a technique for hiding from people.

You Can Come Out of Your Shell

Feel sorry for turtles! Some of them live to ripe old ages, but spend their whole lives in a shell. There's just nothing they can do about it!

If you're shy, you're luckier because you can do something about it. You can come to a better appreciation of your good qualities, you can recall moments when you were proud of yourself and see them once again, you can learn to live with your weaknesses. You can readjust your image of yourself, truthfully, positively. Once you feel better about yourself, you won't be too frightened to come out of your shell.

Did you ever see the birth of a chicken? The cracking of the shell, and then the little chick coming into the world for the first time?

If you're timid, you can be like the little baby chick and burst through the shell into the daylight—into a brighter world than you ever knew existed, the world of friendship, the best world there is.

Before you're ready for real friendship, however, you must have the courage to burst through your shell.

The Meaning of Friendship

A word of warning: There is much friendship these days that is political and insincere.

Some people use "friendship" for vocational advantage, selecting and shedding friends with rapidity and without real feeling. They shop for friends as they would for an automobile, looking for a bargain, figuring out in advance which friend will help them advance their career.

As they achieve promotions and rise into a new social status, they then feelinglessly discard their old pals and begin hunting out new alliances, which are more likely to pay off in terms of cold cash—present or future.

These people do not basically differentiate between one person and another, but make their choices after a careful survey of the economic advantages involved.

Other people select friends and make efforts to cement these "friendships" in an attempt to make others think them popular. Their reasoning is that if people see them always in the company of this person or that, on apparently friendly terms, they will be considered socially acceptable. They think of this as a success, though it really isn't.

They don't really care, in a compassionate way, about the

people they use for their social prestige. Indeed, they use them with the same degree of concern that one would feel in washing dishes or polishing the family car. Their only concern is that their ally be a superficially acceptable commodity, a person with enough status in the community to enhance their own social prestige.

Obviously, no genuine value inheres in these forms of "friendship." There is nothing beautiful or ennobling about these selfish alliances, and I am writing about an entirely different type of relationship, one in which the main ingredient is not expediency, but brotherly love. This honest, giving kind of friendship is one of the most precious things in life, and it is this warm brotherly-sisterly relatedness that I hope I can help you achieve.

Making People Seek Your Company

If people really like you, you won't have to go out and look for friends; not only will they seek your company, they will come clamoring after you.

Let's try out our mental picturing apparatus again. Sit down, make yourself comfortable in a quiet place, and relax in the playhouse of your mind.

Scene 1: This man goes to a party. He knocks timidly on the door, feeling uneasy because he won't know many of the people. Ted was invited by Cora, whom he knows casually in the library where he works. He's 35, has worked as librarian for almost ten years, is lonely. The hostess greets him and he shuffles into the living room which is crowded with talking, laughing people.

"Hello." A girl comes over to him and smiles.

He returns her greeting, wondering nervously what he should talk about.

"What's your name?"

Ted introduces himself, forcing himself to ask hers and feeling all fingers and thumbs as he wonders what to do with his hands.

"What do you do?"

"Oh, oh, here comes that question again," he thinks, groaning inwardly. "I'll have to tell her I'm nothing but a librarian." His shoulders slump and he avoids her gaze as he answers her.

(Here is a sure blueprint for failure. This man's basic quality is a self-hatred that tramples all his intelligence and his potential for creative expression. He must strengthen his self-image before he is ready for the warm givingness that constitutes friendship.)

Scene 2: It's the same party, half an hour later. John arrives and greets his hostess. He's also a librarian; it's a clannish gathering. He's also in his thirties, unmarried, but he's looking forward to the evening. He's eager to meet Cora socially and see her in a pretty dress. Perhaps they'll dance and talk and flirt, and perhaps he could take her home later.

"How nice you look!" he says to the hostess, meaning every word.

He laughs as she blushes and shakes hands with Peter and Frank, both of whom he knows at work. They're glad to see him and bring him over to other people.

"What do you do?" one fellow asks, glass tinkling ice in his hand.

"I'm a librarian," John says, looking curiously, yet with a friendly smile, at the other man. "I've always loved good books. What do you do?"

He finds some of the people at the party interesting to talk to, and enjoys the exchange of ideas, the food and drink. People come over to chat with him, enjoying his easy friendliness, and his lack of pretension and arrogance. At midnight, he takes Cora home.

(People seek out this man because his self-image is healthy. He sees himself as a nice guy and therefore does not have to feel self-conscious or apologetic. Liking himself, without being narcissistic, he is able to appreciate others. They sense this and cluster around him, as bees around honey.)

Your Self-Image Can Make You Likable

You can learn a lesson from these dramas: a healthy self-image can make you likable to other people.

People crave good company. They may mask this desire because they're afraid of rejection, but they feel this need very deeply. It is a basic need, almost as essential as the need to appease one's hunger with food.

Next time there's a fire in your neighborhood, observe the people in the street. Go with them as they rush to the scene to watch the fire engines come clanging up the street and the firemen go rushing out with hoses. Notice how they cluster together, talking animatedly to each other as they watch the firemen put out the blaze.

Chances are, if you're observant, that you'll sense that, more than the fire, they're interested in taking advantage of this opportunity to talk to other people—even complete strangers. Any emergency situation gives people this chance— to group together with many people, feeling somehow more full, more whole.

If your self-image gives you the strength to be a considerate person, you will never feel starved for companionship.

You Can Put Others At Ease

> Friendship! mysterious cement of the soul!
> Sweetner of life and solder of society!
> —Robert Blair

If you give yourself peace of mind, you can tranquilize other people, sweetening their lives and cementing the potential good-heartedness in their souls. You can help them live restful, yet animated lives. If they feel that you accept them as they are, without need for pretense, they will come out of their shells and reveal genuine, wonderful qualities that they usually hide from other people, who they fear are hostile to them.

Francis Bacon once wrote, ". . . A principal fruit of friendship is the ease and discharge of the fullness and swellings of the heart. . . ."

If people trust you, they will confide to you their most terrible fears and guilts, easing their burdens, giving them more energy to direct into positive channels. If you are an accepting person, you can bring them a sense of relaxation that few others can bring them.

If you can help make life sweet for just two or three friends whom you cherish, how fortunate you will feel!

Friends Can Make You a Bigger Person

Many people spend their lives hunting around in what they see as a jungle. Occasionally they cut through the underbrush to some buried treasure and rush it to the bank before other beasts of prey can sink their claws into it. But their lives mainly consist of "dog-eat-dog" adventures. Competitors surround them and they choose their "friends" for strategic purposes.

In *Understanding Fear In Ourselves and Others* (Harper & Row, 1951), Bonaro W. Overstreet writes: "Sometimes we know people who live to be old without achieving any identification that takes them far beyond themselves. They may form any number of overt relationships, may hold jobs, marry, rear children, join clubs. Yet they never actually identify with anyone. They can only use people, cling to people, dominate people. They may profess love—in the proper setting, even love of mankind. But people remain for them means to ends. They never affirm anyone as real in his own right."

This is pathetic because real friends can make your life so rich. In the warmth of your life-giving interaction, you can discover qualities in yourself that you never knew existed. You can become a bigger person through giving friendships.

A friendship makes demands on you; you must give consideration to your friend's needs as well as your own.

In the words of Emerson, "Friendship should be surrounded with ceremonies and respects and not crushed into corners. Friendship requires more time than poor busy men can usually command."

Do not concentrate so much on your materialistic needs that you crush your friendships into corners! What material goods are more valuable than a good friend? Give time to your friendships, and you will receive wonderful dividends!

If you are an openminded person, capable of appreciating all kinds of people, you can receive many rewards from broadening your friendships.

In the Feb. 1960 *Reader's Digest* ("Have You Made Any New Friends Lately?"), Vance Packard writes: "Some people contend that we are happiest when we stick to "our own kind" in developing friendships. The person who wears blinders of this sort will never experience the enthrallment of having as companions such colorful and often vividly articulate individuals as clam diggers, turkey farmers, house detectives, lumberjacks, seamen or antique refinishers. He'll never know the exhilaration that comes from the discovery of someone exciting in a seemingly unlikely place. . . .

"Another reward that comes from broadening your friendships is the new insight you gain from people who have a different perspective. One day I had a long ride in a Boston taxicab with a jovial, elderly driver. We had chatted on a variety of subjects when he suddenly exclaimed: 'You know I have achieved the supreme happiness! I'm glad I'm doing what I'm doing, I've learned not to fight my background. I'm glad I'm who I am.' "

Five Rules for Winning Friends

Apply these concepts and you will never lack friends:

1. *Be a friend to yourself.* If you're not, you can't possibly be a friend to others. If you downgrade yourself, you can still admire other people, but your respect will be tainted with envy. Others will sense the impurity of your friendship and will not respond positively to it. They may be sympathetic toward your problems, but pity is not a strong foundation for friendship.

2. *Reach out to people.* This is the next step. When you're with a casual acquaintance and you feel like talking, express yourself as uninhibitedly as is proper for the situation. Don't tell yourself that you're silly if you crack a joke, or unstable if you're nervous and want the other person to like you! Look for the other person's positive qualities and try to bring them

out; watch for overcritical thoughts and stamp them out, for they are enemies to friendship.

3. *Imagine you're the other person.* This mental picturing will help you. If you try to image him in his total life situation, as accurately as you can reconstruct it, you can sense his needs and try to meet them as much as is within your ability and within the dimensions of your relationship. You can also understand his responses better. If he is touchy in certain areas, you can try to avoid stepping on his toes. When you feel like being generous, you can attempt to build up his own self-image. If he is a worthwhile friend, he will be grateful for your kindness and will be giving to you in return, in his own individual way.

4. *Accept the other fellow's individuality.* People are different, especially when they're being genuine. Don't try to alter this fact! The other fellow is not you; accept him as he is and he'll value you too, as you are, if he's worth his salt. It is a serious mistake to try to force another person to conform to your preconceived ideas. If you resort to such domineering tactics, you'll likely have an enemy, not a friend.

5. *Try to meet other's needs.* Too often this world is a cutthroat place in which people think of their own needs—and then stop thinking! Go out of your way to be considerate and you'll be a valued friend. Many people talk *at* people; they deliver lectures and the other fellow is just an ear. Never do this to a friend; talk *to* him!

Practice Exercise No. 7: Your Self-Image with People

I've offered you some of the wisest advice you'll ever read on winning friends and if you will apply these concepts effectively, your relationships will have a new vivacity that will thrill you.

Your self-image is the prime factor. When you are with people, your feeling about yourself will influence your thinking about them and your conduct in relation to them. This is inevitable.

If you feel you're basically worthless, you may distort your thinking into one of these patterns:

1. You will withdraw into a defensive shell (defending yourself against yourself), inhibiting any spontaneous actions and frowning on spontaneity in others.

2. You will wallow in overcritical thoughts about people, lifting your own weak ego but destroying any chance of friendly relating.

3. You will become gushingly talkative, making a frantic effort to prove you're not worthless (an accusation you've made against yourself).

4. You will be constantly competitive, always trying to knock the other fellow down and pull yourself up over him in status.

I'm sure that you recognize people who relate in these ways, making friendly relating difficult. You yourself may rely on one or more of these defensive mechanisms. If you do, it's time that you strengthen your self-image when you're with people so that you can relate more naturally, without taking something away from others.

As you sit quietly, work on this practice exercise.

Tell yourself that you were made in God's image, and that He fashioned you to love your fellow man and to live at peace with him. You were made to be warm and human and these qualities are in you somewhere, even if it is not superficially apparent.

Remember the simplicity of your childhood friendships. Picture in vivid detail, as best you can, things you did with your childhood friends, possessions and feelings you shared. Recapture your favorite moments of early friendship, imaging the events. Regain the feeling that you can be spontaneous and alive, that you can throw off the burdens of overcivilization.

Concentrate on the loving feelings you have felt for people during your life. Forget the hate and the disillusion! Start off afresh and bring back into your memory your feelings of gratitude for something nice your mother did for you, or a considerate gesture made by your father. Bask in the warm glow of bygone birthdays when people indulged you and in the shared confidences with trusted friends. If your life has been hard, concentrate on the isolated cases in which you felt genuine gratitude to other people. Keep your loving feelings alive as you would a fire to keep you warm, for they are the whipped cream, the champagne, of your self-image. Without the active feeling of love in your heart, life is incomplete.

Reject from your mind emotional scars. We all have them but if you dwell on them, you will undermine your chance to grow in the world of people. If you are a person who spends his time nursing grudges, you can't think very well of yourself without being unrealistic.

Accept your imperfections. If you expect too much of yourself, your self-image with people will be weak. You'll always be looking over your shoulder to see if someone has noticed this fault of yours, or that mistake. In addition, you'll expect others to measure up to your impossible standards and they will feel that you are unaccepting. Once you accept yourself as you are, you will find it easy to give quiet friendship to others and one of life's most wonderful experiences will be yours.

Some of you may have had few friends during your lifetime and feel you're unlovable. This is not so; your trouble is that you've not been fair to yourself. There is something lovable in everyone of us—it just has to be brought out.

Your pride in yourself and your friendliness to others is something that you have to bring out for yourself. No matter if it's difficult; only you can do it. Go over and over the material in this practice exercise and help yourself to grow in stature in the world of people.

14

Finding Peace of Mind
in a Troubled World

When you wake up in the morning, perhaps you open your front door and reach down for the bottled milk and the daily newspaper.

Perhaps you carry the milk to your refrigerator, shut the door, sit down in the kitchen chair and unfold the newspaper. The headlines shriek out at you in large black type—of nuclear weapons, diplomatic threats, individual crimes, government abuses.

"There," you may say, "there's proof positive. You can't relax in this world. There's too much trouble everywhere and it's gotten out of hand."

You're wrong. You can relax. You can create peace of mind—even when others reel with anxiety.

Tension is nothing new. The world has seen many troubled days throughout history. Strife has always been part of the fabric of civilization, from the Greco-Roman wars of antiquity through the bitter French Revolution to the world wars of the twentieth century. The Industrial Revolution brought about disquieting change. No period in American history was more chaotic and senseless than the mid-nineteenth century, when our great Civil War forced fellow Americans to kill each other. Some soldiers even had to kill personal friends of more peaceful days.

No, tension and catastrophe are not unique diseases singling

176

out twentieth century man. There have always been difficult crises to cloud the sunnier part of life.

You can learn to live with these pressures, and even to win out in life's boiling pot. Your life is not worthwhile if you cannot attain a feeling of quietness. You *must* bed down with your soul and breathe in gentle tranquility.

In the words of the great Greek philosopher Plato, "Nothing in the affairs of men is worthy of great anxiety."

In Chapter 3, I gave you some hints on how to relax, but the subject is so urgently important in today's high-pressure world that I'm also devoting this chapter to the vital area.

You Can Learn to Be Calm

First off, you must believe that a state of inner calm is a realizable goal. This may not be as easy as it sounds; if you're used to having harassed, jumpy, pushing people around you, you may come to think of calm as an unattainable state.

Our leading magazines and newspapers feature articles describing the inner turmoil of today's teenagers, the explosiveness of their tensions.

Our most respected social scientists tell us of the abnormal anxiety that pervades modern day life.

Philosophers, psychiatrists and religious leaders agree that people today live without spiritual quiet, full of conflicting emotions, disturbed by resentment.

Millions of people torture themselves with anxiety. Indecisive and fearful, they cannot accept their feelings or their shortcomings. It is difficult for them to make up their minds about anything, and they feel guilty over what they regard as their failures in life. They act too impulsively—or are afraid to act at all. Anxiety becomes a way of life for them. Phobias and neurotic obsessions fill their minds, instead of feelings of success and confidence. I know people who have never enjoyed a really calm *week* in *years*.

Are these further evidence that serenity is beyond your grasp? It is not. I mention these sordid states to show you once again that if you are anxious, you are not alone. There are conditions today that encourage anxiety. Therefore, in your fight to become calm, start off by accepting your anxieties, not blaming yourself for them. The more secure your self-acceptance is, the more you can come to peace with yourself, with your weaknesses, the more attainable is the goal of calmness for you.

You can be calm; believe me. This chapter is full of suggestions that will help you to reach this goal.

Tranquilizers for the Spirit

First, go toward activities that bring you contentment. This is highly individual. Certain hobbies or rituals serve as "spirit tranquilizers" for some people, but would only bore others.

An old lady, a friend of my family who passed away several years ago, told me that when she felt jittery she used to read her Bible. That would settle her nerves. She would just rock back and forth in her chair and read.

A friend of mine, a doctor who would come home tense from the pressures of his practice, would find tranquility in playing the piano. He played mostly Chopin and Gershwin. Sometimes I'd go over to his apartment, light up a cigar and relax with him as his hands flitted agilely over the keyboard.

"I don't know what it is," he once said to me, "but when I'm playing the piano, I relax and just forget the pressures of life. I just enjoy myself. I stop worrying about patients who are in pain, I forget the ones with incurable diseases. Maybe this is wrong of me."

"No," I said. "You've got to relax and forget even your most pitiful cases, or you'll be no good as a doctor and you'll be unable to help the people you can make better. The piano gives you peace—accept this gift!"

You all have your spiritual uplifter—potentially. Find out what it is—and then take advantage of the good it does you!

You Can Master Your Worries

Are you a slave to worry? If you are, ask yourself this: Do you believe in slavery?

This is not a joke. If your mind travels from one worried thought to another, it is truly enchained. You are not a free man.

Do you say, "But there is so much to worry about"?

You don't have to itemize your problems: I grant your point. But this is a negative way to use the wonderful power of your mind.

In *How to Relax in a Busy World* (Prentice-Hall, 1962), Floyd and Eve Corbin write:

"If you have been in the habit of inviting negative thoughts —jealousy, envy, resentment, and self-pity, think of these as intruders in your mind. The old Chinese saying fits here: 'You cannot stop the birds of the air from flying over your head, but you need not let them nest in your hair.'

"Face and define your troubles. Gather knowledge about them from every good source. Confide your worries to God. Do all you can about the situation that is causing them. Don't contaminate your friends and loved ones with them."

This is good advice. Worry is one of the most destructive scourges of mankind; if it takes over your mind, your days will be miserable and your nights will be intolerable. Even if the worst misfortune should befall you, it is no worse than a worried mind.

The famed philosopher Soren Kierkegaard once wrote, "No grand inquisitor has in readiness such terrible tortures as has anxiety and no spy knows how to attack more artfully the man he suspects, choosing the instant when he is weakest; nor knows how to lay traps where he will be caught and ensnared as anxiety knows how, and no sharp-witted judge knows how to interrogate, to examine the accused, as anxiety does, which never lets him escape. . . ."

These ideas will help you master your worry:

1. *Bring your fears into the open.* Talk about them to friends without hiding details which may be ridiculed. The more you express your fears the less serious they will seem to you and the sooner you will forget them.

2. *Seek solutions to your problems.* When you feel you've done your best to solve a problem, even if you haven't found a clearcut answer, you'll feel better about yourself and will be more inclined to allow yourself the privilege of relaxation.

3. *Guide your thinking into constructive channels.* Once you've done your best to alleviate some trouble, thinking about it will only make it worse. Use your imagination more positively, picturing happier situations, or undertake activities that will give you pleasure.

How to Spot Your Over-reactions

We all have our Achilles heel, areas in which we feel vulnerable. Some people fear traveling by airplane intensely, but are perfectly at home behind the steering wheel of the family car. Others feel exactly the opposite. Some people fear neither planes nor cars, but hate to cross crowded streets on foot.

Over-reactions, if unchecked, can undermine your peace of mind. They can remove your thinking from channels appropriate to the realistic circumstances and distort it into patterns that bear no relation to reality.

Dr. Peter J. Steincrohn tells a story of over-reaction *(How to Master Your Fears):* "The year was 1929. Mr. Smith was worth a million dollars just before 'Black Thursday' of the market crash. A month later he had only a hundred thousand dollars. What did he do? Most of us have read of the many such Smiths who jumped from hotel windows. But the average man said: 'Imagine jumping with a hundred thousand dollars in your pocket. I was left without a nickel to my name and you couldn't have pushed me out of a window.' There you have what we like to call normal and the abnormal reactions to a difficult situation."

How do you spot your over-reactions, preventing them from upsetting your calm and plunging you into difficult situations? The best way I know is to talk your situation out with two or three trusted friends, explaining your reactions as you go along. They will, in most cases, be able to see the objective reality far better than you will and they'll be able to help you get back on the ball, planning a new day of full living.

Delay Your Response

Sometimes you will not be able to help yourself and a flood of anger will pour into you, threatening to overwhelm the calmness you've worked so hard to maintain. At such times delay your response, hold it off, and count to 12 (an even dozen).

Suppose, for example, that you live on a tight budget. Any unforeseen expenses that pop up endanger your sense of economic security. You over-react in this area, so that any annoyances of this sort will trouble you even more than is realistic.

You're sitting quietly in your favorite chair, smoking your pipe, digesting a tasty dinner. Even the newspaper headlines please you, giving promise of income tax savings, and no commercials interrupt the pleasant music from the radio. Your ten-year-old son has just brought home a report card full of excellent grades. You just sit and let your imagination wander through fields of rich mental pictures.

Then your wife says that the kitchen linoleum is worn out and the TV picture is blurred. You feel irritated at the thought of expenses, but you are not thrown. Then she reminds you that your $180 dentist bill hasn't been paid. Now the anger starts building and you know you can no longer check it.

This is the time to start counting slowly, "One . . . two . . . three. . . ." By the time you get to 12 you may still be irritated but your rage will be more subdued and you'll be better able to control your actions.

This delay may prevent you from giving vent to explosive destructiveness. You may be able to regain control of your rational faculties and resume channelizing your energies in more positive ways. You can go back to enjoying your pipe, visualizing the more pleasant enterprises which will follow the payment of your bills.

A Pleasant Room in Your Mind

When you were a child, did you have a favorite room to which you went when you were unhappy with the rest of the world? Maybe it was furnished cozily, with soft-cushioned chairs and throw rugs and your most treasured possessions.

This is what each of us needs—a serene room in his own mind—a retreat in which to nurse one's wounds when the strains of the world become unbearable. In the seclusion of this peaceful chamber in our mind, we can recuperate from life's fast pace, refresh ourselves for the new day to come. In this little mental compartment you can make peace with yourself, accepting your insecurities, re-picturing your most cherished memories, setting your present goals, imaging a future full of life, faith and hope, free of resentment and worry.

As you've done while reading this book, you can build a stage on which you can imagine real-life dramas, the kind that will help you to the creation of a self-image strong enough to allow you to lead the good life.

Take a Daily Vacation

As a boy, I knew adults who worked 60, 70, 80 hours a week; this was quite common in those days. Today most people work 35 or 40 hours and Saturday is a day off. They have at least a two-week vacation every year.

Even so, many people feel tense nowadays because of the pressures they *feel* under. The truth is that the length of the work week seems to have limited meaning in relation to one's ability to relax.

What is important is that you take a *meaningful* vacation, and that you take it *every day*. Not once in a while, but *every day*. Every day take a flight into the freedom you can give yourself in the quiet room of your mind.

Birds have long been symbols of freedom and poets have envied their ability to rise above the confinements of earthly existence as they soared through the skies.

In the serene room of your mind, the soaring range of

your imagination can give you this sense of freedom. You can temporarily escape from the shackles of civilization, reaffirm your convictions and return to the realities with increased vigor.

You can take this wonderful vacation if your imagination is your friend, if your self-image is healthy enough to allow you this luxury. Keep sharpening these potent tools as you read this book, and as you re-read it. Then you'll be able to take a wonderful vacation every day—all expenses paid.

Do You Belong to Mañana Unlimited?

These tools for relaxation are not meant to be excuses for laziness; ideally, they will free you to function more efficiently. Do not become a member of Mañana Unlimited!

What is Mañana Unlimited? Mañana in Spanish means "tomorrow" and Mañana Unlimited is an organization that leaves things undone until tomorrow. It is the world's largest organization with more members than any religion, political philosophy or industrial organization. To join up, you must cling to one glaring fault: the tendency to put things off until "tomorrow." Millions slavishly follow this blueprint for failure for a lifetime. Colleges give no courses in it because its learning is instinctive and does not lead to advancement.

This doesn't mean that we shouldn't believe in the art of leisure, which is totally different from putting things off. Idle people have the least leisure, for leisure is the reward of work and feeds the body and mind to meet the demands of tomorrow. As Thoreau said, "He employs true leisure who has time to improve his soul's estate." The man who leaves things for tomorrow hasn't time for improving anything, and this uselessness is emptiness.

Mañana Unlimited espouses a negative philosophy of failure because no one has ever seen tomorrow. We indulge in wishful thinking when we believe that tomorrow will bring a Utopian state of affairs free of trouble. However, we can constructively plan for tomorrow, looking ahead for ways to better ourselves instead of tying ourselves to techniques which will leave us marking time, wallowing in a vacuum.

Therefore, every day we must strive to break away from our membership in Mañana Unlimited. We must break away from the oppressive hold of fear, hatred and worry which make us charter members who stay lazy and say, "Well, we'll take care of that detail tomorrow." We must send in our letter of resignation.

Say to yourself every day: "I will do something even better than that tomorrow. I will improve myself tomorrow, and will try to be more sincere with others and with myself."

But, more important, forget about tomorrow completely. Start improving yourself today, *now!*

Don't Be Afraid of "Escapism"

Some people frown on the word "escapism." It's as if they're saying, "Face up to it! To escape is cowardly!"

To live a happy life, you must come to grips with reality; anything else is an evasion and a misuse of your productive energies. But it is a fatal mistake to feel that this is a 24-hour-a-day task! If you take yourself this seriously, you will be always tense. You will be able to tackle your problems more forcefully if you are able to relax and to reinvigorate yourself with restful sleep. Sometimes "escaping from it all" can be a big help to the busiest, most successful person. Don't be afraid to "escape" and don't look upon it as a waste of time!

I'm most certainly not discussing harmful, self-destructive escape mechanisms. I recommended to you wholesome, positive escapes from pressure: Into the peaceful room of your mind, To the healing calm of the country, Into the intoxicating enlightenment of travel, To the soothing caress of music.

These and other escapist devices are refreshing to your soul and, properly used, will not harm you. They will give you nourishment that will ready you to function more effectively in our swift-moving world.

The Peacefulness of the Country

In 1798, the great English poet William Wordsworth wrote these beautiful words:

> ". . . and again I hear
> These waters, rolling from their mountain-springs
> With a soft inland murmur.—Once again
> Do I behold these steep and lofty cliffs,
> That on a wild secluded scene impress
> Thoughts of more deep seclusion; and connect
> The landscape with the quiet of the sky."

They celebrate the calming effect of Nature, the solace that it can bring a troubled human being. They sing of the comfort one can find in Nature's vastness.

These days expanding industrialization has cut swathes in our countryside, but our country is still blessed with large areas of natural beauty, which is ours to enjoy. There is something healing about being close to Nature and I know many people who drive, tired and tense, to the country on Friday night and come back to the city Sunday night soul-satisfied and bright-eyed, ready for a week of productive work.

While it's true that we can't always rush off to the country when we feel that fenced-in feeling, we can go into the quiet of our minds and picture the glories of Nature that we've seen. These sweet images can help us relax.

Changing Your Surroundings

Sometimes a change of pace can do you good, and this is why many people love to travel. New images, of known or unknown places, bring refreshment to your mind, just as eating a delicious new dish brings satisfaction to your palate.

Travel can sometimes help you solve your problems. Suppose you have to make a decision. You keep weighing the pros and cons, but the more you think, the more tired you feel and you're farther from a definite conclusion than you were when you started thinking. At such a time forcing your thinking will only harm you. You need to escape from the problem for a while; you need relaxation before your mind is ready to go to work again. A weekend auto trip, a few days in strange surroundings, with interesting sights to see and no pressing responsibilities—this prescription might put you in shape to make a good decision a few days later.

The Soothing Salve of Music

Another tranquilizer of the spirit is music. Good music is readily available and its effects are beneficial, yet many fail to take full advantage of this lovely art. The word "music" is so synonymous with qualities of sweetness that Shakespeare once wrote critically of "The man that hath no music in his soul."

Psychologists have recently noted the soothing effects of music. Studies of industrial concerns have revealed that music increases the efficiency and contentment of working personnel. Studies of mentally disturbed individuals have credited music with exerting a quieting effect on them.

Today, many restaurants pipe in calming music to make meals more pleasant for their customers and even some skyscraper elevators have pleasant melodies to soothe the up-and-down journey of bustling city dwellers.

One of the world's greatest composers of all time, Ludwig van Beethoven, was deaf when he wrote some of his masterpieces, but his love of music was so great that he could feel and hear the notes in his mind. All you have to do to hear good music is flick a radio dial and try several stations—or put some records on the phonograph. Don't be too lazy to give yourself an hour of softness when you need it!

How to Find Inner Calmness

"But I want first of all—in fact as an end to these other desires—to be at peace with myself. I want a singleness of eye, a purity of intention, a central core to my life that will enable me to carry out these obligations and activities as well as I can. I want in fact—to borrow from the language of the saints—to live 'in grace' as much of the time as possible. I am not using this term in a strictly theological sense. By grace I mean an inner harmony, essentially spiritual, which can be translated into outward harmony."

These beautiful lines come from Anne Morrow Lindbergh's *Gift From the Sea* (Pantheon, 1955) and they signify the author's understanding of a basic concept in any individual's search for happiness: the "inner harmony" that means so much.

In *Peace of Mind* (Simon & Schuster, 1955), Joshua Loth Liebman expresses similar ideas. "Slowly, painfully, I have learned that peace of mind may transform a cottage into a spacious manor hall; the want of it can make a regal park an imprisoning nutshell.

"The quest for this unwearied peace is constant and universal. Probe deeply into the teaching of Buddha, Maimonides, or a Kempis, and you will discover that they base their diverse doctrines on the foundation of a large spiritual serenity. Analyze the prayers of troubled, overborne mankind of all creeds, in every age—and their petitions come down to the irreducible common denominators of daily bread and inward peace. Grown men do not pray for vain trifles. When they lift up their hearts and voices in the valley of tears they ask for strength and courage and understanding."

Liebman, in this truly compassionate passage, emphasizes the importance of "inward peace," a life goal worthy of any man. The man who attains this quality has found the key to living.

How do you find this inner calmness? It is all up to you—and your self-image.

If you hate yourself, your thoughts will whiz by in your mind with the speed of auto racing cars and you'll have trouble even knowing what you're thinking. You will have to deceive yourself and run away from yourself, and running and running is not restful.

If you accept yourself as you are, with all your human frailties, then you are well on the road to calmness—and happiness.

If you *see* yourself in a favorable light, if your *image* of yourself is pleasant, if this *visual concept* of yourself cannot be shaken by temporary defeats, then you have reached the goal achieved by only the fortunate.

This image of yourself is powerful, more powerful than any words in the dictionary. When *you see* yourself as a success, as a nice guy, ignoring imperfections yet staying close to reality, your conceptual image has great power—and this brings you calmness.

I've given you other suggestions which will help you achieve peace of mind. They are effective and I hope you'll try them out with wisdom, but in the final analysis it is the strength of your self-image which will bring you real calm.

You may feel like saying to me, "I've always been tense. Life has always seemed tough. I've had my share of bad breaks and I worry a great deal and don't know how to stop."

If you're implying that relaxing is not easy, I must agree with you. I have no prescription that will take immediate effect and give you "relaxation ever after." The main point is that no matter how high-strung you've been, no matter how long you've felt this way, you can feel peace of mind—and in a fairly short time.

You can learn to see new *truths* about yourself, erasing old falsehoods which you have taken for truths. There's something good in you, all of you, that you do not realize. I cannot write this often enough, so solidly entrenched are the inferiority feelings of so many people.

There's a very touching passage I came across recently in Lowell Russell Ditzen's *You Are Never Alone* (Henry Holt & Co., 1956):

"In childhood we are first introduced to the feeling of 'aloneness.' We come into the world helpless and dependent, and adjustment to new environments and experiences is never-ending—as poignant in later years as it is in our youth. And not often can we reach across these years to help those who are just starting out on their journey through life.

"Marguerite Bro tells of a child away from home writing to her mother. 'Mommie, I'm lonesome. Deep down inside I'm terribly young and afraid. I feel so unsure of myself and so helpless.' These words might be written by an individual at 80 as well as eight."

188

So many people feel this way—lonely, frightened, helpless. Peace of mind seems far away.

But it's not. As you read this chapter and re-read it, as you go through this book and work on the practice exercises again and again, as you understand more and more your responsibility to yourself, you will gradually begin seeing yourself more accurately—and more kindly.

You will strengthen your self-image and, with it, find calmness.

15

You Can Live Fully
at Any Age

At the age of 65, or shortly thereafter, many men retire from their lifework. Some do it voluntarily, looking forward to some hazy, unrealistic dream of living out their years in a land of sunshine reclining under a coconut tree. Others are forced by society's rules to give up their jobs, which often represent their most dynamic contact with life.

"Retiring" is, for many, a negative concept; it is contrary to living. It is one of the worst words in the English language. After retirement many men deteriorate rapidly. Feeling that they are no longer productive members of society, they feel they are no longer worthwhile human beings. They feel bored with inactivity and feel that they just don't count. Their self-image is negative; that of useless, unimportant nonentities. Many even die within a few years of their retirement.

Retirement from Life

Retirement from their jobs seriously injures the self-esteem of many men; retiring from life and its dynamic pursuits literally kills them. How horrible to spend one's last years sitting on a park bench waiting for death! How negative it is to fear death anyway; the person who has lived zestfully, enjoying each day, accepts death as part of God's plan for life.

The man who retires from his job at about 65 should first substitute other activities which will take its place. He should plan to fill the emptiness in his days, so that they are still productive. If he has creative resources, or if he develops them, his retirement years could be vintage years, devoted to things he always wanted to do but for which he never had the time.

For the man of 65 can still grow up in areas which he never explored. There are always new worlds to conquer, new life to experience, new ways to give of yourself to life and to people.

So, if you must retire, plan for it. Not listlessly, pessimistically, but with a gleam in your eye. Resolve to go on living— for life is not just for the young in age, it is for the young in heart.

"Retiring" Is the Opposite of Living

If you "retire," period, you are giving up on life, instead of embarking upon an era of continued growth. Never give up!

Take myself. I've been a plastic surgeon all my life, but I know that sooner or later—I'm over 60—I'll have to stop practicing. So 15 years ago, I started taking writing seriously. I may be old as a surgeon, but I'm only 15 years old as a practicing writer. I chose writing as a new life for myself to avoid the unhealthy aspects of retirement. When I'm working on a book, I feel young and full of enthusiasm, giving the best I have in me, always trying to improve. I feel as young as I did when I was a kid of 15, playing baseball with my friends or trying to learn more about the world.

Each of you is a unique individual, endowed with your own special interests and talents. Some of you older people can become stamp collectors or book collectors; some of you might enjoy gardening or nature study; some might join social clubs or paint watercolors. You know your latent resources; dig out the gold, throw away the waste products.

I know one man, a veterinarian working as a meat inspector for the government, who was forced into retirement after almost 40 years on the job. Instead of moping, he joined a discussion group, took an active part in it, won popularity as a contributing member of the group, and now moderates its discussions. Never before a public speaker, he now lives dynamically in an area that was never before a part of his life.

Another man, who started working when he was a poor kid of 14 and has spent his life working in the wholesale food products field amassing a fortune, found himself retired at 65. He had never had the time to get a formal education; a wealthy man, he didn't even know what a paragraph was and had read less than a dozen books in his lifetime. These last few years he has spent as a "schoolboy," getting the education he'd previously missed out on.

Don't Retire from Your True Self-Image!

When you "retire," you retire from your true self-image. You destroy a self-image that has taken a lifetime to build; you put yourself in a concentration camp, making an underprivileged inmate of yourself. Faster than George Washington cutting down the cherry tree, you slash your self-image to ribbons. You surround yourself with barbed wire, make yourself the victim of brutal jailers, snuff out your life force in a gas chamber. No secret police come in the middle of the night and enforce this indignity upon you; you do it to yourself.

How can you be of consequence to yourself and others if you do this? In this book I hope to help you improve your self-image and free your creative life forces, so that you can get more out of life.

What I did, you can do. I'm past 60, but when I write I'm young. As I sit in the playhouse of my mind and hold the mirror up to look at myself, I feel that my self-image is youthful. Some days I practice as a plastic surgeon, some days I write. But whatever emotional hardships there are in writing, every day has a goal, something to look forward to. So, at my age, I put a revitalizing cream on the face of my self-image, manufactured by the factory of my desire and will in this field.

And look, a miracle! I have turned back the clock. I'm past 60, but I feel each day the zest of a boy of 15, who has bright days ahead of him. And this is realistic, for my days are bright and I live them as if I've found the fountain of youth. I have, and I'm happy to share my secret with you.

And, if I can do it, so can you!

You're as Young as You Feel

You're 65 now so you've arrived at middle age, you're still in the prime of life; new horizons lie before you and the future is yours.

"What!" you say. "Maybe you didn't hear me right. I said I was 65, *not* 35!"

I heard you. You're 65, and you think you're old, and lots of people think you're old, but you're not. I'm in the same boat as you and, as I've told you, I'm young. I wake up in the morning and I see the sun shining. The sky is blue in my world and the birds sing *and people live*. I eat a hearty breakfast and I don't gulp it down absently. I *eat* it and enjoy it and plan a constructive, life-filled day.

You, too, can be young, and I don't care what your chronological age is. There are people who are old at 21, because their self-image is dried up. And there are people who are still young in spirit at 80. Bernard Baruch and Winston Churchill come to mind.

Don't live by the book! Write your own book of life! Often we think ourselves into old age. Expecting to grow old at a certain age, we prepare ourselves for negative goal images. Tapering off on both physical and mental activities, we lose both the flexibility of our joints and the life force of our minds and spirits. With this type of attitude, one naturally becomes old.

But today a person of 65 is middle-aged. Advances in medicine are increasing life expectancy and diseases which are dread killers today will be curable tomorrow. Furthermore, increases in the scope of Social Security coverage are making it possible for older people to live more comfortably for many years.

So, if you're 65, enjoy your middle age and if you're 75, enjoy your old age. Take part in life and feel young, no matter what your age. Give to life and it will give back to you and you'll feel that life is good.

Naturally, there are limits. It goes without saying that you don't play basketball when you're in your sixties and you don't run the mile at top speed. But at the same time, proper exercise is good for you all your life; why should you ever give up walking or swimming? Keep your mind fertile and your body useful and you'll feel young all your life.

More Living: A Prescription for You

If you get the flu, perhaps you'll see a doctor and he'll prescribe some medicine to help speed your recovery.

I'd like to repeat my prescription for people of retirement age, who suffer from the disease of apathy and lethargy: More life!

The whole business of living is to remember that every day is a composite lifetime for the person who is happy. A day must have a beginning, a middle and an end, and the whole must be harmonious.

Those who are happy look forward each day with faith and hope to realizing the goals that they set for themselves. Each day there must be goals related to life and the society in which we live—no matter how simple, they are basic. For the woman the goal might be baking a cake, while the man's aim perhaps is to bicycle through the park.

Don't laugh at these goals, for if these people have their hearts in what they're doing, the activities are important. To the man, his bike is a symbol of living. Enjoying his movement through the park, he is emotionally going somewhere. Standing still, you may fall down.

It is in doing nothing, in being bored, that people die inside. Did you see the motion picture "Marty"? This is a fine, realistic film showing young people who are old—because they sit around with time on their hands.

Retirement from life is criminal because it's self-inflicted. You become a traitor to yourself when you walk away from your daily goals, denying the life force that God has given you. Age is no excuse at all.

When you retire from life, you walk away from reality

and self-respect, write off your self-image and voluntarily isolate yourself in an inner concentration camp. You put your soul in jail.

Some of you probably think that money represents the solution, but experiments on the problems of living longer have indicated otherwise. Researchers interviewing over 1,000 people of 50 and over have found that money was not a key factor in the happiness of older people. A retired industrialist earning a six-figure income and a man who retired on Social Security checks were found to have identical problems. Preparation, vitality, interest in the contemporary world, work, an ability to take pleasure in others—the researchers found that these were the things that made these people happy.

In short, these trained observers found that people were happy who went toward life.

The Editor Who Retired from Life

A few months ago I had lunch with the editor of a men's magazine and he told me about another magazine editor he knew who had been forced to retire from his job because of his age.

They threw a retirement party for him and all the higher-echelon folks showed up. There was plenty to eat, even champagne, everyone showered praise on him and then—retirement.

For years his colleagues had admired his dynamic dedication to detail and the intelligent flexibility of his mind. His productive ability grew with the years and was still growing when, because of his age, he was forced to retire.

One day after the party, he was like an old shoe, thrown away after years of service.

Today he is a sick man, mentally sick because his productive powers are dying inside him, denied creative expression. After 35 years of dedicated work for his company, this was his reward.

How much better to have allowed him to continue on the job he loved instead of compelling him to retire! Some more understanding firms make retirement optional, and I take my hat off to them.

The Doctor Who Found Youth

Another man, a surgeon, worked at a New York hospital till he was 65, and was then asked to retire. I know him well and for a while he was depressed and moody. This was not like him at all; he was the kind of person people liked and I was used to seeing a smile on his face. But, for the first time in many years, his self-image had taken a setback. He felt that he was no longer useful.

A resourceful man, he got a new job lecturing at a college. Today he is a professor on the medical faculty and delivers stimulating lectures on the background and history of medicine and on methods of surgery. He has regained his feeling of youth and is alive with his students.

Living Fully All Your Life

Today more thought is being given to the problem of compulsory job retirement as enlightened people realize the trouble it can create. Some firms make retirement optional.

In *Live Better After Fifty* (McGraw Hill, 1953), Ray Giles states that "public health authorities, leading geriatricians and others specially interested in the problems of aging are putting themselves on record as against compulsory retirement at 65. . . .

"At national conferences on problems of aging, outspoken criticism is being voiced against hard and fast retirement policies. The economic waste to the nation is being pointed out. . . .

"Statistics prove that in many occupations older people commonly outproduce younger employees. Older employees, statistics show, are more reliable, have fewer accidents and are less often absent from work. . . ."

Don't let your age keep you from remaining on the job if you are allowed your free choice! On the other hand, if job retirement is voluntary and you feel that you can live more fully without employment, then retire and do all the things for which you've never had the time. The thing to remember is that only *you*, in the final analysis, can decide what's best for *you*.

But whether you *must* retire or *choose* to retire from your job, remember, once again: *First prepare yourself in new areas of living.*

In *Ways and Means to Successful Retirement*, Colby Forrest outlines many helpful suggestions for activities after retirement. Your librarian can recommend other books that may give you ideas for enriching your retirement years.

There are organizations in almost all communities which offer activities designed for older people: community centers, YMCAs, settlement houses. They have much to offer you; why not take advantage of their facilities?

Private social work agencies will help the older person with his individual problems, no matter what their nature. So will the religious leaders in your neighborhood church or synagogue.

These people can help you fashion a new, refreshing life for yourself after you've retired. But your main tool is your own self-image and your determination to keep it bright and shining. If you have pride in yourself and if you *feel* that you're young and still attractive, you will create from deep inside ideas with spirit and goals that move you. When you wake up in the morning, you will feel like tasting more life and *you will feel youthful as long as you live.* You will be a living example of what God meant when He created the human race.

There's a funny story in *Live Better After Fifty:*

"In January 1953 Henry Bailey Little looked back over his 55 years as president of the Institution for Savings in Newburyport and vicinity and came to an important conclusion. When his board of directors asked him to serve another term he declined. He said the time had come for a younger man to take his place. So William Black was made the institution's new head.

"So far this doesn't sound very exciting. Actually it was interesting news because the retiring Mr. Little was 102 years old and the 'younger man' chosen to take his place was 83."

Perhaps the moral of this story is: *Life begins at 83.* It can, you know!

Don't be taken in by movies whose heroes and heroines are physically young and handsome or by TV commercials featuring young people without a wrinkle on their foreheads! They are not the only important people around. You—if you're older—count as much as they do and God created each of you in His goodness.

Wine is not good until it is aged; it mellows with the passing of the years. It can be like this for human beings. Young people may be able to race effortlessly around tennis courts and may be capable of dancing around a ballroom all night without tiring. They may climb mountains and swim oceans. But they often lack understanding which comes only through the experience of many years of living. They make tragic mistakes, products of their inexperience. And they often lack compassion and wisdom.

If you're older, you've had many successes and many failures. It must be this way—no life is perfect. Don't dwell on the failures; picture your proud moments. See yourself at your best and admire your self-image! If you do, you will never shrink from life; it will hold no terrors for you. You will live fully all your life, living each day the best you know how, going to sleep peacefully when the day is done, dreaming pleasant dreams.

You will live fully after 65 and as long as you live— with goals, with friends, without self-pity, without resentment, without regret. Loving life, you will never retire from it— as long as you live!

16

Your Daily Dozen:
12 Ways to a New Self-Image

You've read most of my book, and I hope you've enjoyed it and improved yourself through reading it and applying the principles I've set forth for you. If you make use of these concepts faithfully, you will be able to change your self-image and your ability to enjoy a full life.

In this chapter, I am summing up the all-important weapons which you have at your command, your "daily dozen."

They are just words outlining concepts, but they pack the kick of an artillery cannon. With one exception: They will not destroy fortresses, but will simply guide you toward the good life.

1. *Truth*. The Greeks had a proverb, "From the gods comes the saying 'Know thyself,'" but your "truth" about yourself is so often *false*. Most people tend to downgrade their abilities, their value as human beings, their assets. Dwelling on failures and overlooking successes, they whip themselves emotionally with an almost sadistic intensity. Is your truth about yourself real—or is it an alien concept divorced from reality and destroying you from within? Learn to see yourself as you really are in your best moments.

2. *Imagination*. What a wonderful tool this can be—but most people do not cultivate it! "The great instrument of moral good is the imagination," wrote Percy Bysshe Shelley,

England's great romantic poet. Joubert claimed that "Imagination is the eye of the soul." Neglected fields will not produce prolific crops; a neglected imagination will not lead you into the green pastures of an abundant life. Learn to use mental picturing to plot for you the way to a better future. Visualize yourself in the roles and situations you have relished; keep on imaging yourself in these successes, over and over, till your "success pictures" blot out your "failure pictures." Make your imagination a friend to be treasured, instead of a storehouse of fears.

3. *Relaxation.* Life is short, and the individual who wastes it worrying throws away this precious gift that God gives you. Benjamin Franklin said, "He that can take rest is greater than he that can take cities." This is true; taking cities involves superior firepower, while taking rest involves a deep spiritual capacity.

Forgive others, for forgiveness soothes the feelings and brings peace of mind. Forgive also because no one is perfect; when you hold a grudge against someone for years, you may be blaming him for an inconsiderate act that you, in your own imperfection, might have committed. Accept others with their human faults and relax with yourself, fallible as you are. Relax with your failures and aim at the achievement of worthwhile goals. And forgive yourself!

4. *That Winning Feeling.* This feeling can move mountains for you if you feel you are a good fellow who deserves success and happiness. I'm not a soothsayer, I have no crystal ball, and I don't believe in palmistry but I can foresee victories for the person who gets that winning feeling, that image of himself in successful roles. In the words of Emerson, "Self-trust is the first secret of success" and when this self-trust is crystallized into an image of winning, it carries a big punch.

The spirit with which you tackle projects, your feeling about the self which performs in the world of reality, almost predetermines the results of your efforts. Once it is a part of your basic personality, this belief in yourself will pull you through crises and, though it may be temporarily shaken, will revive you if catastrophes befall you. As long as you keep stoking the fires of this feeling, you are rich. You feed your automatic success mechanism, and it produces for you.

5. *Good habits.* "Men acquire a particular quality by constantly acting in a particular way," wrote Aristotle. Your habits, added up and consolidated into a whole, are you. If they are positively oriented, you are a person who goes toward success. If they are pernicious, you are stalking failure. The great Roman poet Ovid believed that "Habits change into character."

Many people believe that you cannot change your habits; this is not so. You can discard bad habits and develop good ones, if you're willing to work hard at change. Re-read chapter 5 for a thorough analysis of this vital subject and learn to question habits that seem almost a part of you and yet are harmful to you.

6. *The Aim of Happiness.* People have different goals. Some are basic, some minor. For example, you may have a basic goal of being a good schoolteacher and a minor one of putting your photo album in order when you get a few hours to spare. As total individuals, people's basic aims vary. Some dedicate their lives to worry or to holding grudges or to obsessive cleanliness. Why don't you dedicate yours to happiness? Think of the feelings that will make you happy, the skills, the successes, the relationships with people, the concepts about yourself, the material accomplishments. Then aim at their realization, keeping this in mind: You must feel that you have a right to be happy; otherwise, consciously or unconsciously, you will put roadblocks in your way. Insist on giving yourself this right: it is your natural heritage. Don't take it away from yourself!

People achieve happiness in different ways. The great Roman orator Cicero thought that "A happy life consists in tranquility of mind" while the Roman satirical poet Juvenal wrote that "We deem those happy who, from the experience of life, have learned to bear its ills, without being overcome by them." Find *your* happiness, don't follow someone else's prescription.

7. *Unmasking.* When you are driving a car 55 miles an hour on one of our thruways, do you wear a blindfold? Of course not. Still, you may go through life wearing a mask to hide your true feelings. This is a blindfold because, in hiding from others, you blind yourself to your potential qualities as

a person. This degree of concealment is so unnecessary; it shows that you think of yourself as an undesirable person: a weakling, or a monster or God knows what. Your truth about yourself is false. When you learn to see yourself with kind eyes, you will have no need for a mask.

8. *Compassion.* This is one of the qualities that separates human beings from beasts—or it should. When you feel for others, deep in your heart, you are soaring to your most wonderful moments as a human being. Others' gratitude may come, in return for your brotherly concern, but your real reward is the warm feeling you will experience, toward others and toward yourself. "Thou shalt love thy neighbour as thyself"—St. Matthew. This love for your neighbor will make you feel good about yourself, about your capacity as a worthy human being. Your meals will taste better, you will sleep better and you will work better if you can feel genuinely compassionate. In the words of Beecher, "Compassion will cure more sins than condemnation."

9. *Accepting Your Weakness.* How would you feel if you occupied a sixth floor room in an office building, and there was no floor? Insecure, naturally. It is like this with people. You may be strong, healthy and successful, but there are no guarantees in life and sometimes everything will go wrong for a while. Your strong self-image will befriend you but, as your troubles mount, you will eventually feel tired and weak. Now the question is, Do you accept your temporary weakness in a human way or do you blame yourself for it, feeling that you're a total failure? This is a key question. If you reject yourself when you're weak, then you have no floor under you and you can never feel secure. Your strength is not real. You are only a "fair weather" friend to yourself, and your self-image is made of paper. Only when you accept your weakness and your strength can you reach your full stature.

10. *Living with Your Mistakes.* "The man who makes no mistakes does not usually make anything." These are the words of Bishop W. C. Magee, and truer words I know not. If you want happiness, you must overcome the perfectionistic streak in you that decrees you must never err. You cannot live with this kind of attitude; you can only cower in a shell

of your own making, afraid to try anything. If Babe Ruth had condemned himself every time he struck out, he would have destroyed his confidence in his ability to hit home runs.

Stop destroying yourself with criticism and learn to laugh gently at yourself when you blunder. If striking out in the game of life doesn't bother you, then you can learn to hit home runs!

11. *Being Yourself.* John Stuart Mill once wrote that "all good things which exist are the fruits of originality." This is a sentence to remember when you feel that you must live your life according to others' prescriptions. Only when you are yourself does your life have real meaning.

Stop basing your personality on the smiles or frowns of other people and give yourself the smile of approval that you need. Strengthen your self-image and others' criticism will just bounce off you without ever getting beneath your skin. Ignore people who try to bully you into submission to their will, understanding that they do this out of weakness. You are truly successful only when you live your life the way *you* wish.

12. *Never Retiring.* Ancient civilizations devised means of measuring time. Centuries, decades, years, months, weeks, days, hours, minutes, seconds. These statistical devices, some people think, tell us whether we are "old or young," but they don't. If you fill your days with activities that excite you, you are young—even if you're 100 years old. If everything bores you, you are old—even if you're 18.

When you approach 65, which society has long labeled a "retirement age," you may be compelled to retire from your lifework. Whether you are or not, continue to lead a useful, interesting life! Prepare some interest before retiring—whether you have children or not—in case you are forced to retire. The time to grow up in one field is when you are retiring from another.

Never go into an artificial state of hibernation that is unnecessary; it will only weaken your self-image!

These are your "daily dozen." Don't be skeptical about them; they will help you to live a better life. When things are going wrong and you feel depressed, read this chapter.

Read it again and again, and you will fortify your self-image. Once you feel better about yourself, you will see the world through different-colored glasses. It will look better to you, and you will look better to it.

17

Rave Notices—for You!

At the beginning of this book, we talked about going into the playhouse of your mind to create the kind of images that will, with effort and intelligence, positivize your concept of yourself and of the world around you.

You can change—but you must be willing to work at change.

As Theodore Roosevelt wrote, "There never has been devised, and there never will be devised, any law which will enable a man to succeed save by the exercise of those qualities which have always been the prerequisites of success—the qualities of hard work, of keen intelligence, of unflinching will."

So work hard in the powerful world of mental pictures, and improve yourself in the world of reality. Make a new, better world for yourself!

Now, go back into the playhouse of your mind once more and relax while I unfold a fascinating story—*about you!*

The Spotlight's on You

Did you ever read in the Bible, "Physician, heal thyself"? You are the only one who can really improve yourself, you are your own physician, and that's why you are the central character in this drama. You are the producer, the director, the chief actor, the prop man. You are going to be in the spotlight.

This is a new role for you because you've always hidden your talents in a closet of fear, buried your resources in a mass of shame. You've always thought so little of yourself that you wore a mask of indifference everywhere you went—so that people couldn't see your "dreadful" feelings. You've always imagined the worst catastrophes befalling you and you've been overcautious about taking chances in life. You've buried yourself in negative habits and have resented those who seemed to be enjoying life.

But you've changed. You're a new person now. Working faithfully on the practice exercises in this book, you've changed one all-important mechanism—your mental picturing. You *see* yourself differently. The pictures in your imagination have become more pleasant; at times they glow. They are not unrealistic; as you have altered your picture of yourself in your mind, emphasizing your successful qualities, you have gradually brought the impact of this new self into real-life situations. Yes, you have changed!

Ring the Curtain Up

The curtain rises and you are on the stage, the center of attention. There was a time when you would have been terrified by this, would have run for cover. Sure, you're a little nervous, but you accept it humanly and don't criticize yourself for it. You don't inhibit your actions because people are watching you. You remain yourself and do not look to the audience for reassurance. You approve of yourself, and that's enough!

Horace, the great Roman poet, once wrote, "Adversity has the effect of eliciting talents which, in prosperous circumstances would have lain dormant."

Of course you have known days of adversity during your life, but these hard times have contributed to your full development as a person. For one thing, you feel compassion for the next fellow, understanding troubles as you do. Your ability to feel compassion makes you a full human being. If life had spoiled you, if you'd always been wealthy and sheltered, your sense of identification with other people might have been blunted.

The audience sees in front of them a growing human being, whose healthy self-image will enable him to enjoy life.

You're a Hit!

Confucius, the famous Chinese philosopher, once said, "In all things, success depends upon previous preparation, and without such preparation there is sure to be failure."

But you needn't concern yourself with failure—you're a hit! You have prepared your thinking for the tasks that will face it. You see new truths about yourself, truths that give you star billing as an individual, that give you the courage to stand out on the stage and be yourself. For this drama is not fictional; you are playing yourself and you're going to have a long run! You'll get happiness from your new role and, if you want it, you'll get money too. You'll make lasting friendships because you are a good friend to yourself, in a wholesome way, and can give to others.

You've Rewritten the Script

The script of this drama is masterly—there's no other word for it. Your heroics equal any Horatio Alger story, as you climb from failure to success.

You will not travel in an absolutely straight line—no one does. There is bound to be some failure even in the happiest of lives. No one is omnipotent; life is not a fairy tale. Success is not a one-way road.

You understand this realistically, and this will help you. Being prepared for occasional failures, they will not destroy your morale. Disappointments may depress you now and then, but you will never again be buried in depression because you have the weapons with which to fight your way out—and the insight to know when to use them.

This is a creative script. You are creating the most valuable state of mind in the world—happiness.

A Lifetime of Living

Your days are now adventures in self-exploration, and in the exploration of the world around you. Your world is a bright, happy place: you like yourself and you have good friends. You work about eight hours a day and enjoy it, relax about eight hours a day and relish it, sleep about eight hours a day and it's not "tossing-and-turning" sleep. When you go to sleep, you're out!

You don't have every little thing you want; such an expectation would be ridiculous. You're not a child who must have every toy he sees; you're an adult with a mature understanding of the imperfections of life.

The important thing it this: *What you really need, you now have.* You like yourself, you can relax with your thoughts and with your friends, you have goals, *your* goals, you are moving toward *your* successes—and you are happy.

Your whole attitude toward life has changed; you no longer are defensive, looking for ways to hide from potential enemies. You have taken the offensive. You go toward life with assurance, prepared for success and ready to accept failure. You feel indestructible because you will not destroy yourself.

Each Day Can Be Joyful

Each day has meaning. You don't just sit around wondering how to pass the time. If anything does bother you, it's that each day has only 24 hours and you have so much living to do.

You're young, like a happy child who fights sleep because he doesn't want to miss out on all the fun he might have had if he was awake.

Every activity has enjoyment. Each meal brings satisfaction, each personal encounter is dynamic, each tree is beautiful, each goal inspires you.

You want to share your joy with others and you feel wonderful when you brighten the life of a human brother. He appreciates your compassion and when you are down, he will try to give you a helping hand.

This is an uplifting drama—*and it is realistic*. Cynics may criticize it, calling it overly optimistic, but a strong self-image can do all this for you. Why need reality be shabby and poverty-stricken? Reality can be beautiful too. Your belief can make it so.

Life Is Yours to Live

You don't always feel strong but it's no crime to feel weak. There are several forms of weakness, one of which bends. The other unfortunately breaks. When you feel weak, you "bend," and then you go on to a reaffirmation of your strength.

Feeling strong, you live dynamically. You need friends more than ever *so that you can give to them*. You need this feeling of giving to others, as an extension of your feeling of overflowing happiness. If you could not find people to give to, you would feel frustrated in the expression of your full sense of happiness.

"Let there be no strife I pray thee, between thee and me . . . for we be brethren" (Genesis).

Your very presence is a reward to your friends, an affirmation of the brotherly feeling of this biblical quote. Your company is a tonic to them because you don't look to tear them down or to compete with them, but to accept them and to make them feel better about themselves. You talk *to* them as individuals, not *at* them as if you were a lecturer and they were your disciples. You feel compassion for their troubles and enthusiasm for their good qualities.

You Are the Master of Your Fate

The world has not changed much. There is still talk about atomic wars and many people are still driven by false gods. But *you* are changed and you have changed *your* world.

You no longer feel helpless. You feel that you are the master of your fate. When you read the morning newspaper and the headlines are disturbing, your agitation does not overwhelm you. If there is anything you can do to better the situation—a letter you can write, a community meeting you can attend—you sometimes may choose to do this. But once you have done everything within your power in the way of constructive action, you forget about it. You do not waste your time worrying; you no longer believe in self-torture.

You go back to living a happy life, setting your goals, achieving your successes.

Your successes become easier as you get that winning feeling. It's like a major-league pinch-hitter who has come off the bench to win game after game. His confidence rides with him as he pictures his past successes and when the manager looks down his bench for someone whom pressure will not upset, he knows whom to pick.

You're not a pinch-hitter, though. You're in the game all the time—you're not a part-time performer. Your talents are well-balanced and your life story could be an inspiration to anyone.

Your drama is a smash success and, as the curtain comes down, the audience breaks into wild applause. You go backstage but the audience keeps applauding, waiting for you to come out and take a curtain call.

Take a Bow!

Now, you step back out on the stage and take a bow. You're the main actor in this drama, the writer and director too, for it is you who have reconstructed your life. I've just been a helper behind the scenes, a production assistant, a prop man.

You've done the real work. You've worked hard on the practice exercises, you've read and re-read chapters that have special meaning for you, you've dedicated your energies to your self-improvement. You deserve all the credit in the world.

The audience applauds again. Most audiences are appreciative and will return good for good. They applaud excitedly, sending waves of love through to you in response to your fine, winning effort.

Change is not easy. It takes work. You've worked and you've changed. You've overcome the skepticism of acquaintances and your own tendency to belittle yourself. You're a bigger person, and this is quite a production. Recognizing this, they continue to applaud until you come out and take another curtain call.

This has been the biggest victory of your life. You are happy with your self-image and need not hide behind defenses. I congratulate you on it!

I leave you with one final wish: that, in the years to come, you continue to *see yourself* as the worthwhile person you are. If you do, you will always be happy!

DALE CARNEGIE—THE MAN WHO HAS HELPED MILLIONS TO GREATER ACHIEVEMENT—CAN HELP <u>YOU</u>!

Start enjoying your job, your personal relationships—every aspect of your life—more fully with these classic books. Check the ones you want and use the coupon below to order.

____ 54435-7 HOW TO DEVELOP SELF-CONFIDENCE AND INFLUENCE PEOPLE BY PUBLIC SPEAKING $3.95

____ 49269-1 HOW TO ENJOY YOUR LIFE AND YOUR JOB $2.95

____ 53267-7 HOW TO STOP WORRYING AND START LIVING $3.95

____ 49891-6 THE QUICK AND EASY WAY TO EFFECTIVE SPEAKING $3.50

____ 49408-2 HOW TO WIN FRIENDS AND INFLUENCE PEOPLE $3.95

POCKET BOOKS, Department DCR
1230 Avenue of the Americas, New York, NY 10020

Please send me the copies I have checked above. I am enclosing $_____.
(Please add 75¢ to cover postage and handling. N.Y.S. and N.Y.C. residents please add appropriate sales tax. Send check or money order—no cash, stamps or CODs, please. Allow six weeks for delivery.) For purchases over $10.00, you may use VISA: card number, expiration date and customer signature must be included.

NAME_____

ADDRESS_____

CITY_____ STATE/ZIP_____ 984

☐ Check here to receive your free Pocket Books order form.

Home delivery from Pocket Books

Here's your opportunity to have fabulous bestsellers delivered right to you. Our free catalog is filled to the brim with the newest titles plus the finest in mysteries, science fiction, westerns, cookbooks, romances, biographies, health, psychology, humor—every subject under the sun. Order this today and a world of pleasure will arrive at your door.

 POCKET BOOKS, Department ORD
1230 Avenue of the Americas, New York, N.Y. 10020

Please send me a free Pocket Books catalog for home delivery

NAME _____

ADDRESS _____

CITY _____ STATE/ZIP _____

If you have friends who would like to order books at home, we'll send them a catalog too—

NAME _____

ADDRESS _____

CITY _____ STATE/ZIP _____

NAME _____

ADDRESS _____

CITY _____ STATE/ZIP _____